WordPress Website Building

101

Everything You Need to Know
to Get Started

About this series

The series "Build And Monetize Your Own WordPress* Website"
includes books and planners written and designed by André Zon.

Books
1. **WordPress Website Building 101.**
   Everything You Need to Know to Get Started.

2. Build Your WordPress Website from Scratch.
   Complete & Detailed Practical Guide For Non-Techies.

3. Create Content and Do SEO on Your WordPress Website.
   Complete & Detailed Practical Guide For Non-Techies.

4. Promote Your WordPress Website Perfectly.
   Complete & Detailed Practical Guide For Website Owners.

5. Maintain Your WordPress Website Perfectly.
   Complete & Detailed Practical Guide For Website Owners.

6. Monetize Your WordPress Website Perfectly.
   Complete & Detailed Practical Guide For Website Owners.

Planners
1. **Website Concept Planner is the companion planner for this book.**

2. Website Development Planner.

3. Content Creation Planner.

4. Website Promotion Planner.

5. Website Maintenance Planner.

6. Website Monetization Planner.

Information and news

Actual information about these books and planners
is published and updated on the websites:

https://andrezon.com - author's site.
Please scan this QR code to open it.

https://buildownsite.com - site of the project.
Please scan this QR code to open it.

Build and Monetize
Your Own WordPress Website

WordPress Website Building

101

Everything You Need to Know
to Get Started

André Zon

André Zon

Build And Monetize Your Own WordPress Website (Series).
Book #1. WordPress Website Building 101. Everything You Need To Know To Get Started.
Edition 2023-2024.

The trademark WORDPRESS is used under license from the WordPress Foundation.

The book uncovers and describes the work required to create a website and for its subsequent operation. The book's purpose is to prepare the reader, who does not have the knowledge and practical experience in Internet technologies, to create a high-quality modern website on their own.

The book's material is focused on using the WordPress CMS, but many of the solutions and tips will be helpful in cases where other platforms are used.

The book is written in simple language. To understand its content, no special training is required. Each topic is accompanied by an illustration that clarifies and complements the text.

The book is addressed to readers focused on creating a website independently or wanting to feel more confident when interacting with professional developers. Also, this book can be helpful for students and those who want to start working in the Internet business.

Table of Contents

About this book

You are not well versed in Internet technologies or have never dealt with or studied them, but do you need to create your own website?

You do not know many things and, therefore, are not confident in your abilities or even know where to start?

You need this book to get through it all and win.

Quite often, the owners of already working sites ask useless questions into the space, experience unnecessary emotions, and are faced with the need to rework what has already been done.

These questions are: "How did it happen that I didn't know about this before?", "Why did no one ever tell me about this?" and "How did I not think of such simple things myself?!".

These emotions are: "Probably I'm not at all fit for this kind of work," "It's too difficult for me, and I'm disappointed," and "I put a part of myself into this work, and it's all in vain!".

These thoughts are: "I'll have to redesign the site structure," "The design is not good because the site pages take too long to load," "I need to come up with something so that visitors do not leave my site so quickly," "My content is not searched because I did everything wrong."

These questions, emotions, and thoughts have at least two things in common.

First, they are utterly useless for business and incredibly destructive to the human psyche.

Second, everything listed above can be avoided if you know how to navigate the subject of creating and operating websites and understand the meaning of each component of these exciting processes.

This book is written to teach you just that.

It is written in simple language. Each important topic is considered briefly but in detail, without unnecessary words. Illustrations complement the text, making it easier to understand.

By reading this book, you'll be ready to start building a website on your own and interact competently with web tech professionals.

Foreword

Dear Reader!

Before you is the first book in a series of guides dedicated to creating, developing, and monetizing websites. This cycle is designed for people without experience creating websites or with no significant experience.

At the beginning of the work, it was assumed all topics could be placed in one book. It turned out that this was not the case. The book would be too, too big.

Therefore, I had to divide all the topics into several parts and start working on a series of books instead of one.

The first book gives an idea of the range of questions that need to be studied and problems that need to be solved. It should be read before you begin the practical creation of the site.

After you have read this book, you can confidently navigate the technical terms and technology of creating websites.

The knowledge you will gain from this book is the foundation without which it is impossible to create websites consciously. It is necessary to understand every required element of the process of building a website and every aspect of its subsequent operation to succeed.

This is a must for building your website, especially if you lack information technology training.

Of course, this is just the beginning. Theory without practical implementation is worth little, and our goal is precisely the practical solution to the problem of creating a high-quality modern website.

The key to successfully creating a good website is to follow the correct sequence of work. This sequence is described in this book.

Based on the material of the books of the cycle, a training project is creating, including an information website, a training website, and various auxiliary information materials.

I hope that all this will help you achieve what you have in mind.

André Zon.

1

How to correctly name the site and choose a domain name

Site title, site name, domain name. With these words, a conversation about creating a new site always begins when its concept has been developed and its functions have been formulated.

But sometimes, it is better to solve all these tasks in parallel. In any case, the choice of a domain name should not be put off for too long.

1.1. Website Name vs. Domain Name: what's the difference?

The title of your site is the title of its short description written in ordinary words. So, it can be in the site directory, business directory, and your business card. In addition, the site name is contained in a particular field on its main page and can be part of the titles of its pages and posts.

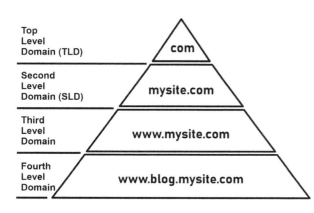

Domain Name Levels

Top Level Domain (TLD) — com

Second Level Domain (SLD) — mysite.com

Third Level Domain — www.mysite.com

Fourth Level Domain — www.blog.mysite.com

The site's name should correspond to its content and purpose as closely as possible. All the words it contains will be the first meaningful words that search robots will see on your site and the main words that will fall into the search engine databases.

This is a crucial element, but it cannot guarantee the complete uniqueness of your site because you do not and cannot have a monopoly on phrases like "clothing store," "weekly review," or "dog hairdresser." Your direct competitors have the right to use such words, and their sites may appear in the search results next to your site or even above it.

Just as important is the domain name you assign to address your site.

A domain name is the same unique website address you type in your browser's search or address bar.

Search robots will see the domain name even earlier than the site name, and this name will be associated with the site forever. Unless, for some fundamental reason, you decide to change it.

Changing the site's name is much easier but does not always give noticeable results.

Changing a domain name is much more challenging, and the result of such a change, as a rule, leads to undesirable consequences.

1.2. What is really a Domain Name?

A domain name is more than just a unique identifier for your website. This is the first thing visitors will see and try to remember. It is the composition of the domain name that can determine the entire future fate of your project.

If we talk about it briefly, a domain name is a string consisting of several words separated by dots. Consider this line, starting from the end.

1.2.1. Domain Name Levels

The portion of the domain name to the right of the very last dot is the first-level domain identifier. The generally accepted abbreviation TLD (Top Level Domain) often refers to it. That is what you will need to choose in the first place.

The next step is to choose a second-level domain name. This is part of the domain name located to the left of the last dot on the line. This part can have a decisive impact on the fate of your project. A second-level domain name is often called SLD (Second Level Domain).

It is the receipt of the selected SLD that requires payment (except in some cases, which we will talk about in other publications) and means the beginning of the life of your project.

There is at least one more level in domain names (in fact, there may be more). The third-level domain name is in the address string between the "https://" characters and the dot separating it from the second-level domain name. Its use is quite common, does not require special costs, and, in most cases, is optional. In some countries, only third-level names can be registered for a site.

If you visit a particular site and don't see anything that looks like a third-level domain name in the address bar, it doesn't mean that the site doesn't have such a name. At least one of its variants exists on every site.

This third-level domain name is known to everyone as "www," an abbreviation for the World Wide Web.

Once upon a time, using various technologies that have long been out of use, this domain name was used to distinguish the website part from other project subsystems that belong to the same second-level domain.

Today, this is no longer necessary, but third-level domain names, if necessary, can be used to access the mail subsystem of the project or the FTP server. In addition, third-level domain names can be used to address individual parts of the project (blog, users, chat, forum, etc.) or site versions in different languages (en, es, de, fr, etc.).

1.2.2. What is important to know about third-level domain names

1. If third-level domain names are used, each address that includes them in its composition will be considered the domain name of a separate site. If these are addresses of versions in different languages, then this is unlikely to interfere with the project.
2. If we are talking about a domain name with "www," this case requires the closest attention. You must take special care to prevent search engines from treating versions with "www" and those without "www" as different sites with different third-level domain names. This well-known problem will be easy to solve at the hosting setup stage.
3. You can add and remove third-level domain names; it will not require money. It's just one way to manage the structure of a project.

2

Top Level Domains:
Types, Features, Choices

Nowadays, the number of domain zones available for registration is considerable, and it is vital not to make mistakes.

A mistake in choosing a domain zone can be very costly, but choosing the right one will save you money and can help you succeed.

2.1. Top-level domain groups

Top-level domains (TLDs), or domain zones, form 4 groups.

1. Infrastructural domains.

There is only one top-level domain in this group - ARPA. It is, rather, a historical landmark because it was with it that the history of the Internet began.

2. Domains of countries and territories, country-coded TLD (ccTLD).

National, country-coded, or ccTLDs are top-level domains representing specific countries and territories. There are 316 of them. Residents of the respective countries can only register many, but many can be used as generic ones. Some are very useful!

3. Generic or gTLDs are top-level domains that do not represent specific countries and territories and do not have a narrow thematic focus.

There are 1249 of them, but only three main ones are the most popular. Each of them has its own purpose. In these domains, finding a domain name for your site is very difficult because many domain names are occupied, including by cybersquatters.

4. Sponsored or sTLDs are top-level domains maintained for non-commercial purposes by government agencies, public organizations, or businesses.

There are only 14 such domains, and only those with the right to do so can register domain names in them. It is possible that one of them may be suitable for you.

The most complete and up-to-date list of top-level domains is always on the official IANA page: https://www.iana.org/domains/root/db.

Domain zones assigned to international brands and zones reserved for administrations and official government bodies are not available for registration.

Note that some domains are marked as "Retired" or "Not assigned" in this list. For us, this means that these domains are currently not working and not being supported, and their fate is unknown to us. Some domains are still listed as available on this official list but are not available for registration.

Top Level Domains

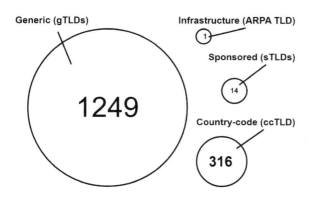

Simply put, when choosing a top-level domain, it is safest to focus on the largest and most famous ones and, in the first place - on the COM zone.

Of course, this is not the only reasonable option.

There is perhaps only one security criterion when choosing a zone - choose a large registrar!

Examine the general list, visit registrar websites - and a solution will be found. For it to be correct, you need to take into account some features.

2.2. Features of top-level domain names from different groups

If your business is local and operates in one country, then the domain name must be registered in the ccTLD of that particular country.

This will give you two benefits:

1. If you have a close competitor whose site is registered in another ccTLD, then for the same search queries in your country, it is your site that will rank higher in the search results (this does not apply to gTLDs that are ranked in the same way compared to ccTLDs);

2. When registering your site in the GMB system and similar business directories, you have a much higher chance of getting approved and much less likely to face additional checks.

In your country and city, it is possible to register and use third-level domain names for addressing the site that has an exact link to the city or state. This is useful for the websites of small local companies.

Some ccTLDs have been used quite successfully as gTLDs, because their names are consonant or just visually close to traditional business areas:

.fm - United States of Micronesia - radio,

.io - British Indian Ocean Territories - IT,

.md - Moldova - medicine,

.me - Montenegro - personal sites and blogs,

.nu - the island of Niue - nudity, and in Sweden, Denmark, and the Netherlands - for business, since in these countries "nu" is translated as "now,"

.tv - Tuvalu - television.

Of course, this is a matter of your choice. Alternatives among gTLDs exist in abundance for many types of creativity and business.

This is just what you need if your business is not limited to one country.

Be guided by the officially indicated purpose of the domain zone and the information of registrars.

Keep in mind that a domain name that matches one of your desired keywords gives you an extra advantage in search rankings and can give you the ability to build a second-level domain name for your site into a meaningful and grammatically correct phrase. This, in turn, will raise the chances of your site obtaining additional traffic and increasing its recognition.

And one more tip: if you want to secure a well-recognized name for your own brand or business, then you can register the same second-level domain name in different zones.

3

Second-Level Domain: this is "Your Site"

At the very least, you will always answer the question about your site's existence with a second-level domain name. The whole world will know about it and call your site by this name.

Choosing the right second-level domain name is not as simple as it might seem. For brevity, from now on, we'll refer to it as "website domain," "domain name," "website address," or simply "domain."

3.1. Choose the right domain name

3.1.1. A domain name is the first thing a visitor to your site sees

A correctly chosen name immediately makes a good impression on the visitor, is easy to remember, and increases the recognition of your project. Ideally, if the domain name is associated with your activity or your brand name.

3.1.2. The domain name should be short and memorable

The simpler and shorter the domain name, the more likely visitors will be able to remember it easily.

A short name is easier to write on any piece of paper. The short name is readily displayed in its whole in the address bar of the mobile phone browser; it can be placed in the header of the site or made into a logo.

All this allows you to show it to site visitors more often and longer, which makes it easier to remember.

3.1.3. A domain name should set you apart from your competitors

If the domain name seems suitable to you but differs from the domain names of competing sites by one or two characters, a hyphen, or is too consonant with them, then it is better to look for another one.

If the similarity is high, visitors may confuse your site with others and not go to your site at all.

After choosing a name, use the search service and check for the presence of "twins" using the keywords included in the domain name.

Right Domain Name

```
            TLD
     Top Level Domain

       • Appropriate

       • Well-known

       • Authoritative

       • Recognizable        .io
                             .tv
     yoursitename.???
                             .com
            SLD              .net
     Second Level Domain     .org
                             .info
       • Short               .club
                             .guru
       • Different
                             .site
       • Memorable

       • Meaningful

       • Understandable
```

3.2. Changing the domain name in the future will be a problem

Changing a domain name is the beginning of a long, thorough, and not consistently successful work. If you keep the old domain name, there will be less trouble.

But they all cannot be eliminated.

3.2.1. The domain name and search rankings

During their existence, domain names receive ratings, reputation scores, and external links.

The domain name is associated with indicators of site performance and the quality of its work.

If you change your domain name, then all this priceless capital will be lost, and you will have to start almost from scratch.

The only thing that can be saved is search traffic if you set up redirects correctly. But even in this case, losses are inevitable.

3.2.2. The domain name and banner ads

If your site is designed to monetize with banner ads from a major operator, then you are almost guaranteed to have trouble getting approval to place ads.

If the content on your site is of high quality and you are not afraid of a possible refusal of such approval, you will lose time to receive it. And with it - and income for the waiting period.

3.2.3. Catalogs, indexes, and directories

For several years of the site's life on the Internet, there may be hundreds of places where information about your project is conscientiously posted, and the site address is indicated.

You will have to restore, find, and update all this information.

But how to update numerous bookmarks in browsers, social networks, publications, and old emails?

You will need to set up a forwarding and solve other technical problems.

3.2.4. Technical tasks for changing the domain name

Here, we provide a typical list of the main tasks that must be solved when changing a domain name.

1. Changing the domain name on the hosting (you may need to purchase a new tariff plan and complete the site transfer).
2. Changing the domain name in the CDN service (registration of a new account may be required).
3. Changing the domain name in the database and service files of the site (may require creating a new site and a complete transfer of content).
4. Change of domain name in Google services (where possible).
5. Change of domain name on linked accounts in social networks.

After that, you need to be patient and observe fluctuations in statistical data. To avoid all these troubles, you must choose and register a domain name on the first try which will not require a replacement.

4

How to choose
a second-level domain name
for your website

The domain name greatly influences the promotion of your site. This applies to both the second-level domain name and the top-level domain name.

The right choice of a second-level domain name significantly affects the recognition of the site and its ranking in search results, the degree of trust of visitors, and all channels for attracting traffic.

Remember that when entering search queries containing words from a domain name, your site will most likely get to the top lines of search results.

4.1. How to optimize your domain name

4.1.1. Use keywords in your domain name

The use of keywords in the domain name is one of the most critical factors in the future popularity of the site and the very first source of traffic.

It is essential that the domain name not only pleases you but is as short, harmonious, and memorable as possible. It needs to be liked by search engines and used when ranking the site in search results. This is why it is desirable to include keywords in a domain name.

Use each search keyword that you choose to include in your domain name only once.

4.1.2. Brand name in the domain name

The brand name should only be used if your goal is to promote it.

It doesn't matter what brand it is - the name of the company, the brand of the product, or the name of the author of historical novels — only the purpose of promotion matters.

Of course, if your brand is well-known enough, then a domain name will serve as good information support for it and strengthen its reputation. If the brand is little known or, for some reason, is not subject to independent promotion, then it is better to look for another option.

Optimized Domain Name

✓ Based on the brand name
bigmikethebaker.???

✓ Based on keywords
spaceshipservice.???

✓ Keywords with obvious digits
24spacegasstation.???

✓ With a hyphen
solar-system.???

❓ With an abbreviation
sssgs.???

❓ With area- or post-codes
onlinestore20318.???

✖ Too many numbers and hyphens
713-281-832-tx-mod.???

✖ With fictional words
dimperwooketlomato.???

4.1.3. Abbreviations in the domain name

If the abbreviation is a brand name, then everything written in the previous paragraph fully applies to it. Coming up with an acronym just for the brevity of a domain name is risky.

You can achieve brevity in many ways. The simplest is to use generally accepted and understandable abbreviations if such an opportunity is found.

In any case, abbreviations should be as short as possible, mainly if they consist of consecutive consonants. And, of course, do not lose the associative link with the site or company.

Especially carefully, you need to combine abbreviations with whole words.

If the brand name is too long, pick one or two keywords that will be associated with your company's activities and used in searches by your potential visitors, and make a domain name from them.

You can bring your site to high positions for queries with these keywords.

4.2. The domain name should not contain anything superfluous

4.2.1. Domain name length

The maximum allowed length of a domain name (a string between two dots) is 63 characters.

Never try to use them all!

When choosing a domain name, follow a simple rule: the recommended maximum length of a string that includes a second-level domain name, a dot, and a second-level domain name should not exceed 15-18 characters. As you consider the various options, try to pick the shortest one.

Here's why you need it:

• it is easiest for visitors to your site and customers of your company to remember a short, meaningful name,

- the name must fit entirely in the address bar of the browser on the most straightforward and cheapest mobile devices,
- if the name is used as a logo, then its length should not deform the page header on devices of different types,
- the name should always read well and fit in the narrow columns of the page layout - in the sidebar and the footer.

Complete visibility and readability are critical for users to remember your domain name.

4.2.2. Letters, numbers, and hyphens

Many numbers and hyphens are often seen as a sign of a fraudulent site. Names with such symbols are remembered much worse.

Try not to use them unnecessarily.

If other options don't work, it's best to make the name a little longer but keep it easy to understand and remember.

4.3. What not to do when choosing a domain name

Here are some more simple rules.

1. Do not strive for excessive originality when inventing words. What seems funny and attractive to you may not always be perceived in the same way by others.
2. Avoid long abbreviations, especially those in which the same or similar letters are placed side by side - this can significantly complicate memorization.
3. Don't forget about the visitors! If you have a local company website, add a designation, code, city name, or area designation to the domain name. And yes, a hyphen might be appropriate in this case.
4. The site's name should, if possible, correspond to the character of the business. For example, if your company is open 24/7, including the number 24 in the site name makes sense.
5. Consider the possible development of your business. Do not include numbers, codes, or other elements in the domain name that will tie the site to business hours or a city if you may move or change work schedules in the future.
6. If you work with an international audience, check the elements of your future domain name - they should not be among the taboo words in the languages your visitors speak.

The next step is domain name registration.

5

How to register a domain name

Registering a second-level domain name in the selected zone is a critical stage in the life of your future website. All formalities of this stage must be taken very seriously.

5.1. What is a domain name registration?

If you have registered a domain name, you have not bought it.

The domain name you created for your site will not become your property after registration.

Speaking formally, you have acquired, for a specific time, the right to administer a domain name.

Of course, such a transaction resembles a purchase, but it does not.

Nothing can be done about it, and there is simply no other way to become the "owner" of a domain name.

Of course, the person who registered the domain name:

- has the pre-emptive right to extend it,
- has the right to reclaim the domain even if the renewal is overdue (no more than the stipulated period - usually up to 2 months - but this may depend on the TLD administrator),
- may retain long-time domain name control if it contains a registered trademark.

In addition, you can pay for domain administration rights (or buy it out, if you prefer to say that) for up to 10 years. By Internet standards, this is an eternity during which you are guaranteed to retain control over a domain name.

Such an order has been developed to resolve the issue of domain name ownership.

5.2. Perform the required domain name checks

So, you have chosen a domain zone (TLD), came up with a second-level domain name (SLD), carried out all the necessary checks, and made sure that the future domain name of your site is:

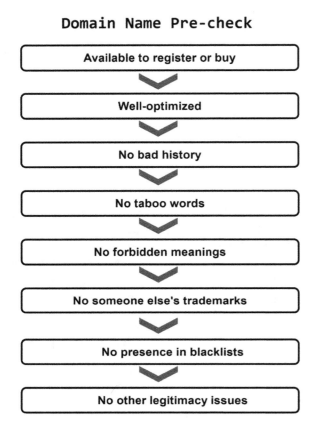

Domain Name Pre-check

- Available to register or buy
- Well-optimized
- No bad history
- No taboo words
- No forbidden meanings
- No someone else's trademarks
- No presence in blacklists
- No other legitimacy issues

• does not have a legally vulnerable similarity to someone else's trademarks,
• does not allow interpretations of meaning prohibited by law,
• does not give anyone grounds to apply to the court for other reasons,
• is available for registration,
• not included in any blocklists,
• has no bad history,
• does not contain taboo words in the languages of the future audience,
• has the right length,
• does not contain (or does include the allowed minimum) hyphens and numbers,
• will not narrow your site's audience when you move or expand your business.

If you have reason to doubt that your chosen domain name meets all the requirements, then it would be best to consult with legal experts.

A domain name is too important to rely on blind luck.

5.3. Choose a domain name registrar company, sign an agreement with it, and register a domain name

5.3.1. What is a domain name registrar

To clarify: you need an accredited registrar. That is, a company that meets the formal requirements of the TLD zone owner, has the necessary technology and equipment, and has entered into an official contract with the zone owner.

To verify the authority of the registrar:
- open the page IANA (Internet Assigned Numbers Authority - the organization responsible for coordinating the main structures of the Internet, the functioning of the DNS root segment, and maintaining IP addresses and protocols used) at the address https://www.iana.org/domains/root/db ,
- find in the list of top-level domains (TLD) the one in which you are going to register a domain name,
- click on the required TLD to open the zone owner details page,

- at the bottom of the page, there is a link (URL for registration services), which will take you to the website of the zone owner,
- the site of the zone owner contains all the necessary information for registering domain names and may also contain the names of accredited registrars if they exist in this zone.

Among accredited registrars, you can choose a company that you are recommended, that you already know, or with which you already have an agreement. In short, a company that suits you.

5.3.2. Agreement with a domain name registrar and other formalities

An accredited domain name registrar is usually a fairly large and reputable company that provides domain name registration services in full compliance with the laws of the country, international agreements, and business rules.

However, for your peace of mind and legal guarantees for the future, you need to follow a series of simple steps:
- create an account on the site of the selected registrar,
- read the terms of service and save them as a printout (or print as a PDF file),
- take a screenshot of your account page so that the page address and the current date are visible,
- fill out an application for domain registration and selected related services, and also save or print the page,
- send an application and pay for it,
- save or print a payment confirmation page, an invoice, and a payment receipt from your bank or payment system.

Keep these documents permanently. When it's time to renew your domain name, repeat the steps above and save all documents.

Also, pay attention to the next point.

Some registrars provide the service of issuing a certificate for the right to administer a domain name. Such a certificate contains all official information and has undeniable legal force.

If your registrar provides this service, then use it.

5.3.3. What to do when registering a domain name

A domain name is of great importance in the business world today and sometimes can carry the same weight as a registered trademark. Few people know, but in the processing of applications for registration of trademarks, in many cases, the consent of the owners of domain names that match their spelling is required.

In short, there are no minor details or trifles in domain name registration. Therefore, domain name registrars provide additional services, each of which can be important for your business.

Additional registrar services can be both paid and free. Be sure to check the prices for such services before registering!

Here is a sample list of such services:
- service of automated selection of free domain names by keywords,
- search for domain names available for purchase from their owners,

- purchase of premium domain names in specialized stores,
- buying existing domain names at auctions,
- buying existing domain names from their owners,
- transfer of domain names between owners without changing the registrar,
- transfer of domain names between owners with a change of registrar,
- registration of a domain name for a long time,
- liability insurance of the domain name owner in case of legal disputes,
- domain name protection by hiding your personal contact information and providing public access only to information about the registrar,
- use of two-factor authentication when transferring or transferring a domain,
- use of two-factor authentication when delegating a domain or changing name servers,
- permanent blocking of a domain name against the transfer,
- domain name blocking for 90 days when you change your payment method or reissue an expired credit card.

Of course, the simplest case is registering a domain name that did not exist before. For it, the list of additional services does not look so long.

We can, without hesitation, recommend that you activate the service of hiding your personal contact information when registering a domain name.

Other services can be provided automatically and without additional payment (for example, blocking the transfer of a domain name) or connected by you at your discretion.

But hiding personal contact information is necessary - you will avoid a lot of trouble from potential intruders and protect yourself from piracy from the very beginning.

In addition, if you have far-reaching plans, then it makes sense to register a domain name for two years or more. Long-term domain names are treated more favorably by search engines.

Your customers will be able to additionally be convinced of the solidity of your business, and attackers may not count on the possibility of an early interception of a domain name if, due to a misunderstanding, you forget to renew it in time.

So, congratulations: you have successfully registered a domain name. We need to move on.

6

What to do immediately after registering a domain name

Your next steps will depend on whether you have a site to which you can connect your new domain name and, in general, on your plans.

6.1. What to do with a domain name immediately

In any case, your very first action is to hide your personal contact information if you did not activate this service at the registration stage.

Find this service on your registrar's website and activate it as soon as possible before information valuable for intruders and spammers gets into their databases. After that, it will be possible to deal with other issues already in a calm mode.

Your second action is to merge variants of the domain name with and without the www prefix.

This action is less critical, but it will allow you to avoid some troubles from the very beginning. In principle, this can be done later at any time, but then you may be surprised that with the www prefix, your domain name can lead to no one knowing where. It doesn't affect anything and is fixable, but still annoying. We will talk about this in the post about configuring DNS records.

6.2. What to do with a domain name if you don't have a website yet

The easiest option is to do nothing.

This option is suitable if you intend to connect your new domain name to a real site in the coming weeks or months.

A domain name, until your site is ready, will not lead anywhere, and there will be no information behind it. Therefore, it will not be of interest to anyone at all, including search robots.

In this case, when your site is completely ready for launch and subsequent work, the life of the domain name will begin directly with thematic content, which will undoubtedly be contained on your site. The first entries in the search engine indexes will be links to your real publications, and everything will be fine.

If you decide to delegate a domain name, that is, connect it to still unused space on your hosting server, then search engine robots will find either an empty document instead of the main page of your site or a ban on visiting it. Both options will not negatively affect anything in the future, but for the first time after the launch of a real site, no one can vouch for the attitude of search engines toward your domain.

If you delegate a domain name and put onto the main page of a website that has not yet been created, the text stating that "the site is under construction," then this text can get into search engine indexes, some lists, and directories. In this case, there is no guarantee that after the launch of the sites, this unnecessary information can be quickly replaced everywhere with the real content of the newly launched site.

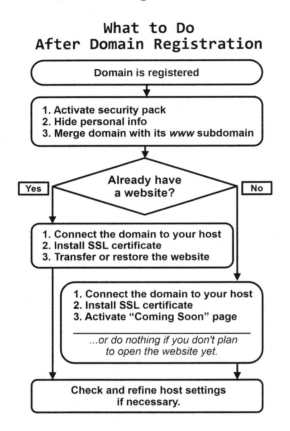

If you do not plan to launch a site within the next months and even years, then look for "domain parking" in the list of registrar services. If your domain name contains popular keywords, then it is possible to make some money from it.

If the domain name was registered as an additional one to the main one, then you can set up a redirect to the main site. In this case, visitors who discovered your new domain by keywords will be taken to your main site, and its traffic will grow.

There is another option for using a new domain name that suits you in any of the above cases if you have delegated the domain: you can connect a mail server to it and use e-mail. This has nothing to do with the website, but we will consider the organization of the mail service in a separate chapter.

The choice is yours.

6.3. What to do with a domain name if you already have a website

In this case, everything is clear.

Connect a domain name to your site, link email services to it if necessary, and go about your business.

What and in what sequence should be done when connecting a domain name to a finished site, we consider separately.

But the work does not end there but only begins.

7

How to connect a domain name to your site: "delegate a domain"

When you connect a domain name to the site, information about this correspondence is distributed to all DNS nodes worldwide, and your site becomes available for visits.

7.1. What is a domain name connection?

First, connecting a domain name technically redirects requests containing that name to a physical server that is reachable at a particular IP address.

In fact, connecting a domain name to a server or, as they say, to hosting is a correspondence between a domain name and a computer with a specific IP address.

When you connect a domain name, information about this correspondence is distributed to all DNS nodes in the world, and your site becomes available for visits.

Technical subtleties and details do not matter since the average site owner does not need to know about them.

Just after "connecting" or "delegating" a domain name, your site, after some time (usually a few hours, the maximum period is 72 hours), starts to be displayed by the browser when you enter the domain name and addresses using it.

Remember that managing domain names and making changes to DNS data are such different things that even when buying hosting and purchasing a domain name from the same company under the same contract for the same account, you will have to work with different subsystems.

7.2. How to delegate a domain name

7.2.1. You ordered a domain name registration service when purchasing hosting services

This is a common practice - hosting companies often offer free domain name registration to new customers.

In this case, most likely, your domain will be automatically delegated to the root directory of your section on the company's server.

**How to
Delegate a Domain**

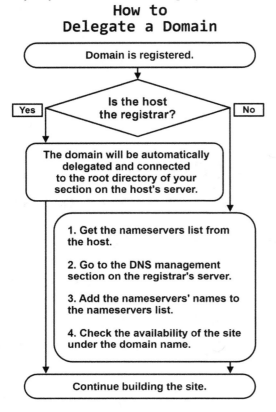

After a short time, you will see that when you enter the domain name of the site in the address bar of the browser, a page will open with the design at the discretion of the host (usually with its logo) and a message like "Something amazing will be here soon!

Don't miss the opening of the site!" or simply "Site under construction."

If, at the same time, the actual site is in the root directory provided to you by the hoster, then after a while, the main page of your site will open under your domain name.

Please note that in this case, you may be able to connect additional domain names, each of which can be used to address a completely separate site.

We will consider these subtleties in a separate chapter in detail.

7.2.2. You registered a domain name and bought hosting services from different companies

In this case, you will need the following:

- in the interface of the hosting control panel, or the documentation for the hosting plan, or as a result of communication with the technical support service, get a list of name servers (usually there are 2, less often - 3 or more) and their names and IP addresses (they can not need),
- in the interface of the control panel provided by the registrar, find the section responsible for DNS management, and in it - the page or dialog for managing name servers,
- add the names of name servers and, if required, their IP addresses to the list on the registrar's website.

Then you need to wait and periodically check the site's availability under the new domain name.

8

How to check the availability of a site under a new domain name

The availability of a site under a new domain name can be checked in four different ways. These methods can be followed step by step.

8.1. Checking on the registrar's website

In the list of your domains, you will see the message "delegated" next to the domain name.

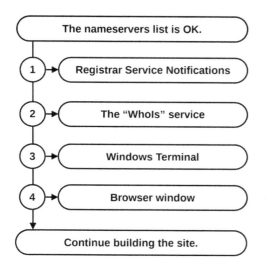

This means that the registrar service checked the DNS settings on the hosting site, successfully checked all the necessary parameters, and did not find any flaws or errors. For you, this means that the problem of delegation is solved.

In this case, the registrar takes data on delegation from its database.

But keep in mind: this does not mean that your site is already visible to the whole world, including you.

The registrar's servers work directly with the host's servers, so they get the result very quickly.

The rest of the world accesses the hosting servers through auxiliary communication nodes.

It must take some time before the information about binding a domain name to a hosting server is updated throughout the Internet.

If the delegation did not take place, and the registrar services sent you a notification of errors, this means that something was done wrong. Usually, we are talking about misunderstandings like a forgotten additional name server or a misspelled name.

The most reasonable thing in this situation is to simply contact the registrar's support service, and then, if the problem is not resolved, contact the hoster.

8.2. Checking by the WhoIs service

It is best to use the WhoIs service on the registrar's website.

A positive or negative test result will be as fast as in the previous option.

The difference with this check is that the registrar, in this case, takes only information from the general registry of domains for which IANA is responsible.

If, during such a check, you see "state: REGISTERED, DELEGATED" in the information about your domain name, then everything is really in order.

If you see the entry "state: REGISTERED, NOT DELEGATED," then you need to return to the recommendations given in the previous paragraph and correct the mistakes made.

After you see positive results of domain name delegation in the registrar's interface and WhoIs service, you can periodically check the status of its availability.

8.3. Checking in Windows Terminal (PowerShell)

Just type the command **ping domainname.zone**
and press the Enter key.

Here **domainname.zone** is your domain name, e.g. *abc.com*, *mysociety.org, . . .*

If all goes well, you'll get a few lines of output that will tell you how long it took to exchange test data packets with your site's server.

If your site is not yet available in your area at your new address, you will see a message like this:
"Ping request could not find host *domainname.zone*. Please check the name and try again."

In this case, just wait a few hours.

After the check in the terminal window gives a positive result, you can proceed to the next, final step.

8.4. Checking in a browser window

Just enter your site's domain name in your browser's address bar. If the site is already available in your area at its new address, then you will see its main page or the hoster's information page.

If the site is still unavailable, then you are still waiting, but there is no reason to worry since all the previous steps have been completed.

It's just that usually, the browser sees the site at the new address as the last one.

After this stage is completed, you can start working directly on the site.

9

Where to look for expired domain name (dropped domain)

Buying the rights to a domain name that previously belonged to another owner can be an excellent deal or, on the contrary, a bad deal.

If you are lucky enough, you can buy a good domain name, which in the past served to address a quality site that is thematically close to your business.

In that case, your future site can begin collecting quality traffic from its first days. Always start your domain name search with the registrar you are working with.

9.1. Using the WhoIs Service

The very first step is to check the availability of the domain name using the WhoIs service.

It happens that no one picks up expired domain names for subsequent resale, and they turn out to be "non-existent."

After the expiration of all the terms provided by the rules, data about these domains is simply deleted from the domain name registry and all services responsible for the operation of the DNS.

In this case, the WhoIs service will tell you that the domain name does not exist.

But this does not mean at all that these domain names and the addresses of pages of an already non-existent site associated with them have been removed from all directories, directories, and search engines.

Therefore, when you get such a domain name at your disposal, you immediately get a certain number of external links, and this can give noticeable advantages when promoting search queries.

It will only be necessary to properly set up redirects so that search engines do not complain about your new site due to the infamous 404 error code.

9.2. Auctions and Domain Name Stores

Large registrars usually provide information about domain names that are expiring or have already expired and services for their reservation and subsequent registration.

To purchase the rights to a domain name you like, you need to send an application to the registrar and pay for booking and registration services.

Dropped Domain Name Features

Looks good	**Sounds good**
Good for SEO	**Safe to buy**

If the old owner of a domain name renews or renews its registration, the registrar will refund your money. If the domain is released, then the registrar will transfer the rights to it to you.

This is a very good way.

Dropped Domain Name Sources

Registrar services	**WhoIs service**
Auctions and stores	**3rd party databases**

Firstly, you do not risk anything, and the registrar takes care of everything.

Secondly, if the domain name is used to address a real site, you can check the content of that site and print the correct solution.

Thirdly, if the registrar monitors his reputation, then the chances of getting a domain name with a bad history at his disposal are much lower than when using the next option.

9.3. Third-party databases of dropped domains

This option may also work for you.

If the dropped domain has not made it to the databases of major registrars, and you are not sure which name is best for you, you can turn to public databases.

Such databases are actively used by cybersquatters, and sometimes interesting options come across in them.

In this case, you should understand that it is safest to register a domain name from a third-party database if such a name is no longer used and not recognized by the WhoIs service.

If the name is still in use, but you need it, then you will have to assume all the risks associated with a possible transaction or use the services of specialized intermediaries.

10

How to check dropped domain

Whichever way you find a dropped domain, it requires checking for several indicators. The main thing when conducting a test is to make sure that for each indicator, the result turned out to be positive.

The recommendations and services listed below may be helpful to you in further work on the site.

10.1. Blacklists

Blacklists do exist, they are different, but each of them can have a bad effect on the fate of the site. No one knows the exact number of such lists since any company can maintain its blacklist of domain names.

A domain name can get into such lists both for real violations and for misunderstanding. If you need the name, then you can think about excluding it from the black lists, but this case requires consultation with specialists.

The easiest way is to simply not take domain names that are on blacklists.

You can start checking a domain name for blacklisting from the Sucuri service *(https://sitecheck.sucuri.net)*.

10.2. Previous content

This is a very important check. If the domain name you need was previously used for a site that is similar in content and subject matter to your site, then this can positively affect the indexing of your pages.

Start checking with the WayBack service. Particular care must be taken to ensure that the domain name never in its history refers to illegal content *(https://web.archive.org)*.

10.3. Domain name history

To check the history of a domain name, use a special service *(https://whoisrequest.com/history/)*.

You can find out a lot of useful information: the history of a domain name from the moment of registration, information about the hosting of the site addressed to it, domains that contain redirects and links to this site, and much more.

This information can be of great help to you in your decision to purchase the rights to a domain name.

10.4. Glued domains

A glued domain name is a name that, along with another name, was used to address a site.

How to Check a Domain Before Buying

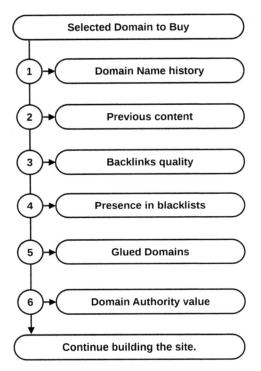

- Selected Domain to Buy
- 1 → Domain Name history
- 2 → Previous content
- 3 → Backlinks quality
- 4 → Presence in blacklists
- 5 → Glued Domains
- 6 → Domain Authority value
- Continue building the site.

There is nothing wrong or illegal with this.

Just sometime after registration, such a domain name will begin to lose reputation, and it will drop to zero as if the domain had never been used.

In this case, you will not receive any benefits from the positive history of the domain name and the relevant previous content of the site referred to by it.

A strong start will be replaced by a fall, and you will have to deal with promotion from scratch. Only in this case search engines will know that there was a period of negative dynamics in the reputation of this domain name. Whether this will affect his future fate is difficult to say.

To answer this question, try starting with the registrar's technical support questions. There, they can tell you which tool is best to use for verification.

10.5. Page Rank

This is one of the common quality indicators not only of the quality of the site but also of each of its pages.

You can get such estimates using the PRChecker *(https://prchecker.info)* and the Moz services *(https://www.moz.com)*.

10.6. Domain name authority metrics

Domain Authority (DA) is an assessment of the quality of a domain from the point of view of search engines.

The higher this indicator, the better the content of the site will be ranked. For a new site, this indicator is 0, and for a large site with global popularity – 99. You can use the Ahrefs service to get this score *(https://ahrefs.com)*.

11

How to buy a domain name from its owner

The domain name buyer is always at a disadvantage compared to the seller.

The buyer pays money, with which he knows the price, for a product he does not know everything about. Sometimes, he does not know the main thing.

11.1. Who can be the seller of a domain name

Most often, it is a cybersquatter.

He can call himself a "domainer" or a "domain investor" - this does not change the essence of the matter.

Quite a few people only need domain names for speculative sales sometime in the future. That is why these people register them.

No websites, no content. On the empty place.

And yes, such people sell domain names expensively.

Of course, such activity has a distinct shade of illegality since registration of a domain solely for sale is formally prohibited. In addition, people often do not like it when someone appropriates possible names for the future results of their hard work.

But what is, is. It is tough and expensive to prove the speculative intentions of a registrant. No one does it except for large brands that have such an opportunity.

However, not all domainers do this as a business. It may well turn out that the domain you need is being sold by a person who registered it for his project, but the project did not take place.

In this case, it is easier to sell the domain name at a cost to recover its registration and maintenance costs.

In addition, it may turn out that the existing project moved to a new domain name, and the old owner decided to sell it.

In general, if someone is selling a domain, buying it for you depends on your financial capabilities.

You will have to pay not only the price set by the seller. The cost of thoroughly checking a domain name is also your concern.

And you need to check such domain names especially carefully.

11.2. Domain name verification

11.2.1. Perform available technical checks

First, you need to check the domain name in the same way as the dropped domain.

Check the history of a domain name, past content of related sites, authority scores, and blacklistings.

In this case, additional check options are available for dropped domains.

11.2.2. Contact the domain name administrator

Try to find the administrator's coordinates through the Whois service. Most likely, they are hidden; today, it is a common practice.

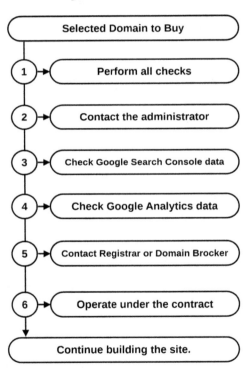

How to Buy a Domain Name

Even if they are open, the administrator may not answer you. In this case, you need to use the services of a registrar or a domain broker (often affiliated with or works directly for the registrar).

You can contact the owner through a registrar or a broker using the registrar's contact information at the address in the results of the Whois check. Just write about your desire to purchase a domain name - and you will be contacted.

In this case, the registrar or domain name registrar broker will negotiate with the domain name seller on your behalf and fully arrange the transaction at a price you agree on.

But before buying, you need to conduct an additional check.

Ask the seller (through a broker) for access to Google Search Console and Google Analytics for the domain name you want. Google Analytics will allow you to verify that there is no low-quality "spam" traffic, and Google Search Console - that there are no manual actions and security problems for this domain.

If everything is in order, you can proceed with the transaction.

11.3. How to make a deal to buy a domain

Our advice: use the intermediary services of a registrar or a domain broker. This will remove a lot of questions and save you from problems. If you try to make such a deal alone, you risk losing money and not getting anything.

You can make a safe deal on your own if the seller, you, and the registrar are in the same city, and you can make a deal in the old-fashioned style - come to it in person and sign all the papers with a pen.

A professional seller, unlike a buyer, usually knows quite accurately for what price a particular domain name can be sold. Bargain with him, and there's nothing more you can do.

The best option for a transaction is under a contract. If we are talking about a significant amount, then hire a lawyer, draw up an agreement on the sale of domain name administration rights, and proceed in the same way as when buying, for example, a car.

In any case - do not try to save on the security of the transaction; contact the professionals.

12

What kind of site do you need?

Consider typical site options and try to determine the requirements for hosting resources that you have to choose. We will proceed from the functions of the future site, the volume of its content, and the expected traffic.

In addition, for future work with WordPress, you must select a "theme" for the site. A website theme is a set of customizable page and block templates that work with a specific set of built-in features.

Many hundreds and even thousands of themes are available to WordPress users, and most are specialized in some way. To navigate this diversity, you need to be able to use the existing classification of sites.

12.1. Types of sites, their features, and purposes

12.1.1. Landing page

Such a site comprises a single page dedicated to one product or service.

On this page, in full accordance with the marketing rules, the visitor is explained why he may be interested in this product and what kind of important information about this product can be obtained, what discounts and special conditions of sale can be provided, and how to proceed to find out the complete information.

Such a page usually contains a small amount of colorful and attractively designed information and quite a few links and buttons that the visitor can interact with.

As the user views such a page, the user is involved in the process of obtaining information and responding to calls to action.

The task of such a site is to receive "leads," that is, the contact information of visitors, which will then be used to send offers and callbacks.

The life of such a site coincides with the life of the product offered, after which the site is no longer needed.

Typically, such sites are actively promoted in advertising networks and receive significant traffic, which can be, for example, hundreds of thousands of visits per day.

For such a site to work quickly and stably, the main criterion when choosing a hosting is the amount of RAM provided since it is primarily consumed during high traffic.

12.1.2. One-page site

This type of site is usually a presentative page of a small local company - for example, a store, an air conditioner repair shop, or a hairdresser.

Of course, such a site can contain several pages if necessary. Still, the amount of information remains small - a brief description of the company, a list of goods and services or a downloadable price list, a small photo gallery, feedback or application form, contact information, and a map.

All this information is quite conservative, so such a site may be updated rarely. The typical structure makes it easy to create such a site, and the choice of themes for this is extensive. The costs will be very modest.

Such a site can be developed in the future, turning it into a full-fledged business site.

12.1.3. Business, or company website

It differs from a "business card" site in a more branched structure and may contain a significant amount of content.

Basic Site Types

1	Landing Page
2	One-page Site
3	Company Site
4	Personal Site
5	Thematic Blog
6	Creative Portfolio
7	Online Magazine
8	Online Store
9	eCommerce Site
10	Community Site
11	Directory Site
12	News Aggregator

Such a site may contain a product catalog with illustrations and certificates, a corporate blog with publications about products and company activities, photos and videos, a forum or chat for customers, sections with materials for downloading, and much more.

In addition, the site may have separate landing pages with special conditions and offers and pages with limited access intended for company employees.

In essence, this is a virtual office of the company, where the visitor can find everything that interests him or contact persons - all the necessary tools for working and communicating with visitors and within the company.

Such sites are usually developed for a long time. The process of their growth and transformation goes hand in hand with the process of growth and development of the company.

During this time, such sites can gain relatively high reputation indicators and rise to high positions in search engines.

Many companies prefer to order the development of such sites rather than using ready-made solutions.

Usually, after some time, this leads to the fact that the site gradually loses the ability to function normally, and it becomes increasingly difficult to maintain it in working order -

simply because the developers changed their field of activity, quit, or stopped participating in the project for other reasons.

This vulnerability is inherent in all long-term projects.

Therefore, sites of this class today can be successfully created based on WordPress or other CMS and maintained in working condition without any problems.

A corporate site usually requires a dedicated server with exclusive use of resources, but you can start with regular hosting as well.

12.1.4. Personal site

It may surprise you, but personal sites are one of the most unpredictable categories. Their range is extensive - from a rarely updated single page to a substantial thematic site, which is inferior to a corporate one, perhaps only in the thoroughness of design (but maybe not).

Such sites are usually created and maintained by people who know WordPress well. These people know how to optimize images, reduce the load on the server, and effectively use various features and tricks.

As a result, such sites can be located on cheap shared hosting and, at the same time, successfully withstand the traffic of tens and even hundreds of thousands of visits per day.

If you are self-reliant in mastering WordPress, have expert knowledge in any area, and can produce a reasonably large amount of content on your own, then this is your option.

All you need at the initial stage is standard shared hosting and an official WordPress site, where you can easily find a minimalistic, light, fast theme and all the necessary plugins.

12.1.5. Blog

A blog is usually primarily a constantly updated feed of posts on one or more topics.

Blog navigation usually uses simple menus of several categories, a tag cloud, and a post calendar.

Such sites are popular among writers, travelers, healthy lifestyle advocates, and people who find blogging a way to express themselves, a way to earn extra money, or simply create and maintain their professional reputation in this way.

Simply put, the owners of such sites are focused on producing a lot of meaningful content. At the same time, they do not have the opportunity, knowledge, or need to complicate the structure and functions of the site. They just don't need it.

Such sites rarely have significant traffic. Disk memory and other hosting resources are also consumed little.

Therefore, blogs usually use the most affordable hosting plans or even free hosting on public hosting platforms.

Creating a blog on WordPress is very simple - perhaps the most significant number of themes has been developed for this, which surprises with variety.

12.1.6. Portfolio

The portfolio is a kind of blog in which images are in the first place, and texts are of secondary importance.

Photographers, artists, webmasters, designers, animators, videographers, antique restorers, soft toy makers, fashion models, and many others - the number of people who need to have their portfolio is hard to imagine.

For this type of site, WordPress has a vast number of themes, as well as all kinds of plugins for organizing a variety of galleries.

The main characteristic of this type of site is a more significant amount of data compared to a regular blog. A professional photographer or videographer can fill any modern hard drive with his materials, so when choosing a hosting, the amount of disk space and the "number of nodes" comes first.

The number of nodes is a term that hosts use to denote the total number of files and directories that were created on the selected hosting. You should pay attention to the fact that the actual number of image files can be 4, 5, or more times greater than the number of images uploaded to the database of the WordPress site.

This happens for one simple reason. When you upload, for example, a photo to a website through the WordPress media upload interface, image processing programs create several pictures of various sizes from it.

This is necessary so that your image is correctly placed in different places on the site page and is not converted on the fly from the original large image.

At the same time, during the site's operation, both the amount of page data loaded and the processor time of the server will be saved.

12.1.7. Online magazine

Online magazine is one of the most popular types of information sites.

Such sites can be thematic collections of articles compiled by one person or online versions of solid, thick magazines.

The online magazine is a large collection of illustrated publications - up to tens and hundreds of thousands and more. It has many categories combined into an extensive menu system. Headers can have their own design, news feeds, various interactive blocks, and more.

Such a site has one main goal: to keep the reader's attention as long as possible, just like a magazine printed on paper.

Interestingly, WordPress is also suitable for creating online magazines. Many themes have been developed for such sites that allow you to create large magazines. At the same time, a small team can easily manage the content of such a magazine since WordPress is very effective for projects of this kind.

A popular online magazine can have quite a lot of regular traffic. It requires a reasonably large amount of disk space and many nodes to host the content.

Pages with complex layouts require many illustrations and decorative elements, which affects their loading time.

Therefore, hosting with a large amount of traffic and disk space is usually required for the successful operation of such sites.

In order not to overload the server, using a CDN in such cases is reasonable.

12.1.8. Online store

An online store is a website for a company that sells goods or services over the Internet.

Such sites are very popular with small and medium-sized businesses that are ready to work directly with customers and buyers.

An online store usually combines a regular corporate business website and a trading system.

It contains information about the company's history, news feeds, a blog, reference materials, and all other types of information typical for corporate sites.

But its central part is the trading system. It has a back end and a front end.

The back end is the database, media collections, and server part of the software. The database contains a category of goods, complete information about goods, prices, conditions of sale, received orders and their status, availability of goods in stock, accepted payments, delivered orders and returns, and much more.

Media collections are photos of products, files of descriptions and instructions, videos, and other files.

The software is responsible for the logic of information processing and interaction with all participants in the processes of filling the store with goods, selling them, and working with payment systems.

The front end contains a closed part, accessible only to company employees, and an open part, with which the buyer interacts.

The closed part is the tools that allow the company's employees to maintain the online store in working condition continuously. Such a store is always open and should work without interruption.

The open part is that tiny tip of the iceberg the buyer sees. Here, you can register an account, find the products you need, put them in the basket, pay for the order and monitor its status, make a return, and contact a consultant for help.

In general, such a site is a rather complex system. Traditionally, such systems were developed on individual projects. Qualified developers were involved in the development.

The cost and development time of the online store were very significant, and maintenance was expensive.

Projects of this magnitude required the involvement of significant resources.

Now everything has changed.

All the functions listed above are implemented in dozens and hundreds of ready-made solutions, constructors, and specialized platforms. Creating an online store takes a few hours, and the launch period is determined mainly by the speed of filling out the catalog.

The WordPress platform has not been left out. There are many solutions for this CMS, the most famous of which is WooCommerce.

This solution, which originally appeared as a fairly powerful plugin, today is comparable in structure, complexity, and variety of functions to WordPress itself.

This means that the launch and content of the online store have become available to everyone who runs a business related to sales.

In this case, most likely, hosting is needed quite powerful - in the form of an administered dedicated server or a specialized cloud solution.

12.1.9. eCommerce site

An eCommerce site is a lot like an online store, except that instead of physical products, it's designed to sell digital products that don't require a warehouse or shipping system.

Digital goods have their specifics. For example, some of them may be provided free of charge for some time or permanently. Others may require you to provide a unique license number at the time of purchase to avoid pirated copies.

But even in this case, we deal with a full-fledged back-end and front-end.

When it comes to selling digital goods, there are many ready-made platforms on the Internet. Most of them are available for free, and any author can sell their digital works on these platforms - photos, drawings, applications, NFT works, music tracks, and much more. Of course, for a commission in favor of the platform.

For individuals, this option is undoubtedly good. But it is not suitable for a serious business in which many people are involved. It is quite natural that there are ready-made WordPress solutions for sites of this kind.

Hosting requirements, in this case, are about the same as for the online store.

12.2. Conclusion

We have not considered such options as community sites, ample thematic resources, directories, aggregators, etc.

All of them, in one way or another, contain elements and blocks that are part of the site types we already considered.

It's just that life is much more diverse than standard schemes and template solutions.

Your modest personal website can grow into a travel-themed resource with its online store, and a small auto repair business card website can grow into a huge website of a specialized dealer center.

It is possible that, having achieved success in business, you will find the opportunity to pay for the creation and maintenance of large and complex sites made on individual projects.

But first, you need to go all the way to success. A WordPress site can be a reliable and undemanding companion for you from the first steps of this path to the very finish. You need to build it right and own it right.

13

Hosting options, or how to choose a hosting company

If you do not understand what hosting options are, then you are simply far from this topic. There is nothing wrong with this. Now, we will talk about the most important things in simple words.

13.1. Basic parameters of virtual hosting

The most important thing to know from the start is that every hosting option costs money in one way or another.

Maybe you just want some redundant features to make your site run faster and more reliably. Or did the manager of the hosting company convince you of this?

Well, there is nothing wrong with that; just pay the bills, and your site will feel great, and you will not suspect that the overpay exceeds 300%.

If you are not burdened by excessive spending, then this way of solving the problem is quite suitable.

Or, perhaps someone knowledgeable told you that you could take a cheaper tariff plan - and everything will work fine, like his. But your site is not working as fast?

You just installed a "heavy" plugin on it and connected a stunning theme your daughter liked because of the dynamic effects and cute icon animations.

So you just made an unbalanced choice instead of finding a powerful enough plan for a reasonable price. Or your new site needs urgent optimization.

And how many more opportunities for the wrong choice!

My advice: if you are not experienced enough, go from small to big.

Any hosting company will appreciate you if you purchase additional resources as the site's capabilities grow or update your tariff plan with increased capabilities and cost.

We will start our journey with shared hosting - the most popular among beginners.

When you get comfortable and gain enough experience, you can determine what features you will need.

Shared (also known as virtual) hosting is the most economical.

Your site will be hosted on the same server as the sites of other hosting company clients and share all of its physical resources with them. How this process is organized is a matter of separate consideration and primarily concerns technical specialists.

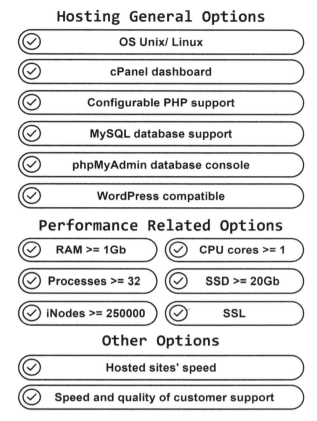

For us, the main thing is to understand what resources are allocated for our site.

Running ahead, it should be noted that when a site hosted on shared hosting starts to consume more resources than it should, the host will notify you about it.

So, you will have a choice: either find an opportunity to reduce the load on the server and stay within the previous tariff plan or ask the host to increase the resources for your site.

In the latter case, you can either add resources of the desired type or purchase a tariff plan with more powerful features. The problem's specific solution depends on a particular hoster's specifics.

First of all, hosting is not only about a website.

In addition to the actual operation of the site, the hosting capabilities for a specific tariff plan also include the ability to work with email, data security services, security features, the choice of installed software, access to various services and settings, and much more.

Consider the main features and parameters in order. First of all, you need to focus, of course, on those parameters that determine the site's quality.

If the site works well, then all other issues can be solved one way or another. If the site does not work well, the solution to all the other problems does not matter.

13.2. Parameters affecting the operation of the site

In this case, we are talking about the implied indicators of the site's quality - overall availability, response speed, page load time, and additional performance indicators.

These indicators have recently ceased to be of an abstract type after the introduction by Google of a system of criteria called Core Web Vitals. These criteria contain exact values for various indicators and can be used to evaluate the quality of work of specific sites. We will talk about this separately; this is a crucial topic.

Now, it is enough to know that not only the degree of satisfaction of its visitors but also the attitude towards the site on the part of search engines and other services will depend on the site's quality. And this, in turn, can affect the ability of the site to attract search traffic.

Overall availability is the percentage of time a site is up and running. Usually, all hosts indicate numbers from 99% to 100%. You can only find out the truth by experimentation. It may turn out that your site just ended up on a relatively busy server. In this case, just contact technical support and ask to resolve this issue.

The response speed is critical. The hoster does not discuss it because he cannot always influence this parameter. We will also talk about this in a separate paragraph. At the initial stage, keep in mind that many large hosts have servers in different parts of the world. Choose a server location that is as close as possible to your future audience.

The first important parameter indicated in the tariff plan is the amount of RAM allocated to your site.

Remember that a single site is currently only available on the cheapest plans of all hosts. It is often possible to have multiple (or many) sites with different domain names on the same plan. But the resources of the tariff plan will be common for all your sites!

So, the amount of RAM (RAM) determines the site's ability to simultaneously process a certain number of requests to the site, queries to the database, scripts, programs, and everything else.

The more complex your site is, and the more visitors interact with it at the same time, the more memory is needed to process requests to the server.

If there is not enough memory, then your site with a large number of visitors may respond slowly or entirely stop working.

Some hosters specify the maximum number of requests simultaneously processed by the server. 32 is enough for an average site, and 64 and above is enough for a complex site with high traffic.

Some hosters indicate the approximate maximum number of visitors per month for the tariff plan. Keep in mind that this is more of an indicative number for a poorly optimized site than a limitation.

For example, if the hoster specifies 50,000 visits per month, this does not prevent you from having 100,000 per day if your site is well-configured.

I know cases, including from personal practice, when a site on a rather weak hosting had traffic of more than 300,000 visits per day for several months without creating any problems for the host server.

It is impossible to accurately calculate the required amount of RAM without information about the server and the configuration of your site, so use simple, practical advice: focus on the amount of RAM 1Gb. If your site becomes very complex and visited, it will not happen immediately, but in most cases, this volume will be more than enough to start with.

CPU Cores - number of available server CPU cores. Naturally, the more the better, but 1 will be enough to get started.

We have considered the parameters that are not only important for the quality of the site but can also affect its fate on the Internet.

Other parameters are also important, and we will talk about them below.

Keep in mind that your hosting management system, called cPanel, has a Metrics/Resource usage section. In it, you can monitor the consumption of your site's resources in real time, monitor their dynamics, and even determine if there are any problems.

Based on this information, you can predict the need for an increase in resources in advance and plan the transition to a more powerful tariff plan.

It is easier to calculate the amount of disk space if you know in advance how many files your site will store. But there is no great sense in this evaluation.

The minimum hosting plans from most hosts offer 20-30Gb of disk space (or more), which is more than enough for the vast majority of sites that can be built on WordPress.

We have already discussed the number of Inodes. This is the total number of nodes, which is considered all files and folders created on the disk space allocated to you.

This includes all folders and files, including files and folders of WordPress itself, installed themes, and plugins. Therefore, the more nodes in your tariff plan, the better. Aim for 250,000 nodes to begin with.

The server should use SSD-type disk storage. Fortunately, this is almost the norm.

13.3. Hosting improvements in the future

Pay attention to the possibility of adding resources without changing the tariff plan. This may be important because this way of adding resources will be done in the background and will not affect the site's operation in any way.

Also, check with technical support and find out what work can be done at no additional charge. In particular, find out how and under what conditions you switch to another tariff plan.

We are talking about sites running on CMS WordPress.

For you to be able to create such a site, choose hosting under OS Unix / Linux, with cPanel hosting control panel, MySQL DBMS with access through the phpMyAdmin program, and PHP language support.

If you want to manage multiple projects and if you need to have more than one WordPress site, pay attention to the following options.

Any tariff plan on any hosting allows you to connect one second-level domain name as the site address. In this case, you will be able to create third-level domain names at no additional cost to address separate independent parts of the site with their help - blog, forum, mail, and various services.

It is also possible to connect various second-level domain names as synonyms (aliases) that will be "glued" with the main domain name of your site so that search engines do not consider that your site exists in several copies under different addresses.

In addition, a hosting plan can support multiple sites.

Then, you will be able to develop several projects on one hosting and later, if necessary, move them to other tariff plans or other hosters completely independently, as separate sites.

In this case, the pricing plan should contain information about the ability to support multiple MySQL databases, multiple domain names, and multiple sites.

13.4. Site Security

A critical issue is the availability of a dedicated IP address.

If your chosen tariff plan includes such a service, this is very good. In this case, your site will not depend on which sites are on the same server as yours.

The fact is that if you share the same IP address with sites that have claims from search engines or spammer blacklist administrators, you will have problems. Your site (and all sites on the server) will not be blacklisted, but restrictions will affect it.

In addition, if neighboring sites, for example, are subjected to DDOS attacks, then the entire server and all sites hosted on it will suffer.

You will not face such troubles if your hosting neighbors behave in good faith.

But having a dedicated IP address is better.

The second most crucial issue is using SSL, which implies access to the site via the

HTTPS protocol.

Today, the use of SSL is an absolute must for search engines. If your site is available only via HTTP, its position in the search results will be low.

But that's not all.

The lack of SSL is a vulnerability that could allow attackers to intercept information transmitted between the server and the browser.

The problem is solved by issuing an SSL certificate. It can be free or paid.

This issue requires separate consideration, but keep in mind that it is a priority, and when choosing a tariff plan, you need to consider the need to address it as a priority.

If your site is not intended for making payment transactions and does not store the critical personal data of your visitors, then a free SSL certificate will be enough for you.

The third important issue is the security of the data of the site itself.

There is only one reliable solution: creating backups that are suitable for its full recovery.

Usually, the tariff plan includes backup and restore service. As part of the programs available through the cPanel hosting control panel, you can find programs designed to back up and restore a site from previously made backups.

As an old-school man who started with punched cards in his hands, I prefer more reliable and predictable methods. We will look at them in more detail, but at the initial stage of work, you will have to rely on the hosting plan. In any case, the promised options for creating backups will not hurt.

The main thing is that you will need to have several powers, without which the full-fledged work of building your website will be challenging.

14

Ways to access hosting resources

You need sufficient access rights to fully manage the site's resources on the server and perform and control essential settings. If the hoster restricts them, fulfilling vital tasks can be very difficult.

14.1. FTP access to the server

FTP (File Transfer Protocol) is a traditional protocol that allows you to upload files to a server, view them, and download them from a server.

This is a convenient access method if multiple people work on your sites.

You still have primary data for accessing the cPanel hosting control panel, and you create logins and passwords for your colleagues to access server folders and define their powers.

You will need to use a special program - the FTP client.

There are many, and some of them are free. In general, if you plan to work with a team, providing the required number of FTP accounts is advisable.

If you're only a solo worker and don't need to move many files between your computer and the server frequently, cPanel's file upload tools may be sufficient.

14.2. Server access via SSH

SSH (Secure Shell) is a special protocol for remote server management and data exchange with it.

SSH access is aimed at experienced professionals familiar with SSH console commands. In this case, they do not need access to the cPanel hosting control panel.

You do not need this method if you work alone and only through cPanel. If you involve experienced professionals in work, then this method can be useful.

14.3. Access to system files and services

14.3.1. *.htaccess* file

You will need direct access to the *.htaccess* file. That's right: the name of this file starts with a dot.

Some hosters artificially limit access to this file since inept actions with it can make the site completely inoperable and even create some problems in the server.

Nevertheless, it is necessary to be able to work with this file. Just do not make changes to it, the nature of which you do not know for sure. And, of course, save a backup copy of this file before making changes.

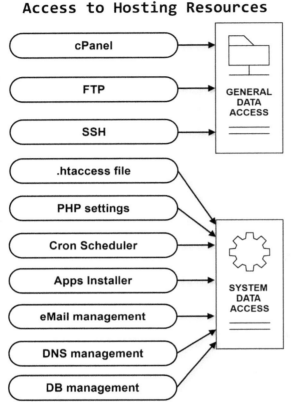

Access to Hosting Resources

In short, this file contains special instructions that control your site's important web server back-end settings.

Full-fledged work with the site is extremely difficult or impossible without access to this file.

We will consider operations with this file repeatedly.

14.3.2. Managing the *Cron Scheduler*

Cron is a program for automatically running recurring tasks on a schedule.

With its help, you can automatically create site backup copies, send emails, and run PHP programs.

Simply put, in order not to manually perform the same routine tasks, the *Cron* service is programmed for its automatic execution according to a schedule.

The cPanel hosting control panel provides a special interface to manage this service.

Keep in mind that this service is not something for beginners. It's possible that you won't need it at all. But if you need it, then you need to know why.

14.3.3. Email Management

Within the capabilities of the selected tariff plan, you can create mailboxes in your domains at no additional charge.

The cPanel panel has tools for creating mailboxes, receiving, sending, and reading letters, and obtaining information for setting up email clients on your work computers.

In addition to Google mailboxes, you can have as many mailboxes on your domains as you like and provide credentials to access them.

Some hosts allow you to use tools for organizing mail groups. This is convenient if you need to manage your mail service, for example, for your employees.

Typically, mail tools include antivirus programs, autoresponders, and other additional apps.

15

Website builder
or your own
WordPress website?

The question at the head of this chapter invariably sparks a holy war. Website builders have their supporters. Various CMS, including WordPress - have their supporters.

Your website, which you have on your own, which can be placed on any hosting, is the best option, according to people who have been doing business on the Internet for a long time.

Which option is the best?

All options are good in their own way. Otherwise, they could not exist. You can choose any of them and successfully work with them. We focus on building your website based on WordPress.

When you finish reading this chapter, it will become clear why we are discussing this option.

15.1. What is the difference?

There is no clear boundary between the capabilities and architecture of websites built using website builders and websites based on CMS.

The principles of creating sites in both cases are the same. Technical composition and logical structure, too. The ability to manage the work of sites, too.

What is the main difference between website builders and CMS?

It is in what exactly and to what extent the site owner can control. The options may differ in small details, but the situation is generally the same.

15.1.1. Limits of control when using the website builder

A website builder is a system that allows you to assemble a ready-to-work website from ready-made blocks without any technical training or knowledge of the creation of the websites.

Now, we are talking about the most common type of site builder, which is combined with hosting and does not allow you to create transferrable sites.

In much the same way, a child collects toys from kits for assembly.

The user has access to an interface that allows you to operate:

- composition of available blocks and functions,
- the visual layout of content on the front end,
- the content of various types.

The back end is not available to the user of the site builder. The service owner takes over all the possibilities of site interaction with the outside world.

The abilities to control a site built on the constructor are limited. Each deviation from the terms of service requires additional payment or effort. In some cases, this may simply be technically impossible because the service owner puts a lot of restrictions on its capabilities for completely objective reasons related to performance and security.

15.1.2. Limits of control for a CMS-based site

Content Management System (CMS) is a somewhat outdated term. From the very beginning, it was too "narrow" and did not reflect real possibilities, but now it is simply used by inertia.

Modern CMS allows you not only to manage content and solve many problems related to the operation, promotion, security, and other aspects of website ownership.

But the site is not only a CMS that allows you to get absolute control over the front end. There is also a backend. Control over it is even more critical when it comes to full ownership of the site.

We will consider a situation where the control over the backend is performing with the cPanel console - the most common, reliable, and easy to learn.

The owner of such a site does not have control only over the system part of the back end.

Site Builders vs. CMS

Features	Site Builder	CMS
Site management restrictions		
Back end	⊗	⊘
Front end	⊘	⊘
Extentions	⊗	⊘
Vital restrictions		
Data export	⊘	⊘
Data import	⊘ ⊗	⊘
Manual backups	⊗	⊘
Host change	⊗	⊘

* Mostly website builders with hosting
** Self-hosted websites with WP-like CMS

The host is responsible for its performance. It allocates computing resources, disk memory, and all necessary services and programs to the site owners.

CMS imposes its limitations, but its capabilities are always greater than any website builder's because CMS developers are not bound by backend resource requirements and try to fill their product as much as possible to succeed in the market.

With all this, the site owner can do whatever they want. He has access to the very most complete control, which is limited only by security requirements and equipment capabilities.

Yet more complete control over your site can only be obtained if the site owner is also a web designer, programmer, system administrator, security specialist, content creation specialist, and promotion expert. But this is such a rare case that it makes no practical sense to consider it here; these are stories for memoirs.

15.2. Website Builders

Website builders are different.

They can be universal, allowing you to create sites for various purposes and of varying complexity. They can be specialized - for example, for creating online stores or creating and maintaining personal portfolios. They can be combined with hosting or be used standalone.

Let us briefly describe the features of the main types of such constructors.

15.2.1. Website builders combined with hosting

This is the most typical case, and it was this that we considered in the previous paragraph.

You buy a resource pack as you would for regular hosting and get access to the control panel. The service owner does not provide the services of the usual classic hosting but specializes in using the website builder.

You are given a choice of site types (blog, shop, restaurant, portfolio, etc.) and a collection of suitable templates that can include hundreds of ready-made templates.

Within the limits of the provided possibilities, you customize the site's appearance and fill it with content. No technical questions concern you in this case.

Additionally, you will have access to email tools, connecting your domain name, and any promotional means. Integration with some social networks and advertising systems is also possible.

In addition to limited control over the site, in this case, you may be accompanied by such phenomena as advertising placed by the service owner on your site's pages, traffic restrictions, and other restrictions objectively due to the capabilities of the equipment and service channels.

In addition, it will be impossible to transfer such a site to another site or even to full-fledged hosting. Transferring the content for use on a new version of your site will also be daunting.

We are not saying that search engines may not be happy with such a transfer; we mean only the technical side of the matter.

The cost of using such services is comparable to the cost of regular hosting.

The features of such a solution also include the typically low speed of sites and the difficulty with optimization in terms of performance and SEO.

If the disadvantages of such a solution do not bother you, and you are ready to use such a service, then this is your choice. Examples are Wix, Tilda, and others.

Keep in mind that you can get a similar service at ***https://wordpress.com***.

The famous CMS runs there in website builder mode, and with free access, you can quickly and easily start learning WordPress.

The interface in this system is much more straightforward than the full installation version of WordPress but very similar.

15.2.2. Website builders based on classic hosting

Many hosting companies, especially huge ones, develop and offer users their proper constructors.

On the one hand, this allows them to compete with popular CMS; on the other hand, it will enable them to bind a client to the hosting service.

So, if you find an option that is understandable to you and suitable for functionality, this may be a good solution.

The hosting companies' proper constructors allow the site owner to gain an advantage over the constructors discussed in the previous paragraph.

You can use a simple and intuitive interface of the constructor. Still, at the same time, you will have access to all the features of traditional hosting with a minimum of restrictions on accessing data and other hosting services.

In essence, you use full-fledged hosting but minimize your efforts in mastering the tools for building a site and further working with it.

In this case, the limitations you will encounter are related to the typical design limitations in terms of capabilities and a relatively small selection of templates for sites and pages.

15.2.3. Website builder as an add-on over CMS

We have not yet considered the features of using the CMS, but we cannot lose sight of such a type of constructor as an add-on to the CMS.

Any CMS (and WordPress is no exception) is much more powerful than other solutions, including the constructor. Therefore, the CMS interface is more complex, and the system's logic is not always easy to understand.

A constructor is a system with implied ease of use.

Therefore, for popular CMS, particularly WordPress, many constructors are installed as plugins.

They provide a simple visual layout of pages, offer many original types of information and interactive blocks, and provide various options for changing the site's appearance.

The real boom in such solutions began after WordPress introduced an alternative to the classic built-in content editor - the Gutenberg block editor. Block-by-block editing has its faithful fans, and solutions such as additional constructors are explicitly designed for them.

The use of such designers is a fascinating process. The creative freedom modern software provides people far from information technology inspires many.

We have nothing against it; only it should be noted that such solutions have the same disadvantages as other constructors.

Firstly, the implementation of the site is tied to the constructor, and subsequent rollbacks, switching to another constructor or abandoning it becomes difficult.

Secondly, your site may significantly lose performance if you are overly fond of various types of original information blocks with many design elements and attributes.

I advise you not to start working with the CMS using the constructor.

It is much more practical to start with the CMS itself and, in the future, if necessary, choose a constructor with an understanding of all the features of such a solution.

15.3. Content Management Systems - CMS

We are supposed to use WordPress as a CMS. We will not consider other systems and conduct their comparative analysis.

Now you will find out why.

Once, back in the early 1990s, I had the opportunity to solve the tasks of producing multimedia CDs in the popular niche of edutainment. For this, both third-party and self-developed authoring tools were used, which are the prototype of the CMS that appeared later.

Then, in the late 1990s, I had to tackle the challenge of developing a whole family of websites for a major publishing house that published weeklies in various cities and countries. For this, a CMS was developed, which perfectly coped with all tasks - from receiving materials to posting them on the regional sites of the system.

After that, it was time to create complex publishing systems, of which, of course, CMS was a part.

Then, after the dot-com boom and bust, I created a website builder that worked like a SaaS.

Then came the era of mobile applications, but work on sites did not stop for a day.

I have had the opportunity to test, use, design, develop, implement, maintain, and refine many content management systems. It is clear that as a result of 30 years of close work on this topic, I have some experience.

This experience allows me to assert that the popular modern CMS is the best thing developed to create websites and successfully operate them for many years. You can write thick books and long articles about them. You can discuss them for hours at conferences, interviews, and reviews.

But we will not waste time on this because it is impossible and unnecessary to work with several systems simultaneously. One must choose one and work with it without wasting time, for life is short.

Whichever CMS I recommend to you, you have every right to ask why this particular CMS. And you will ask, users always ask this, and I have heard this question hundreds of times.

Therefore, I will not get involved in the discussion. Take it for granted: in most cases, you should use WordPress. If you've read this far, then this is your case.

Here are the main features of WordPress that distinguish it from competing systems.

1. WordPress surpasses other systems in terms of the number of users by dozens of times. This means that it is not just a successful but a very well-tested system. This is a very stable CMS with well-debugged and well-functioning code.

2. The vast majority of hosters provide technical support for WordPress sites. This means that you will not have difficulty solving any technical problems. Many hosts even offer special hosting plans for WordPress sites.

3. WordPress allows you to create sites of almost any complexity and purpose; no significant restrictions exist. This applies to design, content, and functionality.

4. This system is easy to install and use for a person who does not know HTML, CSS, PHP, and other languages and technologies.

Like competing systems, WordPress assumes complete user control over hosting resources, the ability to transfer the site to other sites, and full compatibility with all related services without additional effort.

More details about this system await us ahead.

16

Does
website design
matter?

The question of the meaning of website design arose along with the first websites. At the same time, the answers to it appeared. The first answer was design is the main thing!

16.1. The evolution of website design

This madness on the outside of the question is characteristic of the era of the first sites.

It's just that no one knew why websites were needed yet, and it was easiest to impress a listener, partner, manager, or investor with unusual content design, original buttons, and menus for navigation or animation, even where they should not be used.

Many years have passed since then.

HTML and CSS standards changed each other, PDAs and specially made PDA pages of sites appeared and disappeared, and the same fate befell WAP technology.

But the design question remained, and it still comes up in connection with creating new websites and modernizing existing ones.

The traditional, archaic understanding of design is also called website design. We won't go into details. Just keep in mind that this understanding remains among people who may not open any sites for years, and if they do, it is only through desktop computers or desktops with high-quality large screens.

It isn't easy to convince such people of anything.

For example, to convince them that in some market segments, the share of users visiting sites from a smartphone has long exceeded 95%.

Today, everyone has already forgotten about "elastic" and "resizable" website pages. The term "responsive" is used now.

16.2. What is "responsive design"

This means that any page of your site should open on any device with a screen of any size and quality so that the content is located as logically as possible, all texts are well-read, and all of the buttons and menus retain their functions and work exactly in the manner as the user expects.

This is the main principle of the design of any site today.

Traditional design elements - colors and fonts - today are responsible for the ease of reading and perception of information.

Dynamic elements still serve as the primary tool for attracting attention, but in the modern information environment, social networks and messengers have largely taken over this function. Why this is so - we will consider this in a separate chapter.

A modern site designed for the mass user, first of all, should be convenient for perception on mobile devices.

This is the axiom of today.

Another conclusion follows from it.

16.3. Website design and speed

For the user to feel comfortable opening the pages of your site on a mobile device, these pages should load as quickly as possible. This, in turn, means that they should not have anything extra, including unnecessary decorative elements (we will consider their harm in publications on SEO).

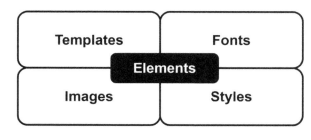

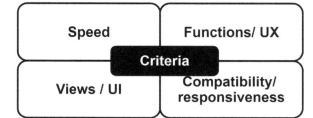

Of course, the desktop version can look arbitrarily busy, but remember that it must have a mobile version that is fast, of reasonable length (if you count the number of screens), well readable, and does not lose functionality.

Your site can have any purpose and any saturation with content and functions. If you want to get your share of the attention of a mass audience, then your site should feel great on a smartphone screen.

The already established appearance of the pages of such a site includes a header area understandable to visitors with a logo, a search icon, a main thematic menu folded into an icon, the main content area, and a footer.

Such a vertical page template gives little creative freedom to the designer.

But you can look at the design problem from the other side.

Is it bad if your site loads quickly and is easily read on any phone? No, it's just great!

Nothing superfluous should be on its pages — only a necessary amount of corporate identity elements, header, main content, and footer. Honestly, nothing else is needed (and never was required).

If you do not have an art gallery website, the visitor does not open it for aesthetic pleasure.

Remember the word "usability"? It is used less and less and has long gone out of fashion. If you think about it, this word denoted the ability of the site (its desktop version, of course) to perform the tasks assigned to it, even though the web designer, guided by the customer's requirements, tried very hard to make this impossible.

This artificially created word nonetheless reflected the site's ability to maintain functionality.

And the design here generally has nothing to do with it.

16.4. What does it look like today

If you want to know this, pick up your smartphone and open the main page of the Google search engine. Or Bing. Or Yahoo. Or of another serious and successful market participant.

Compare what you see with what I wrote above and try to find the differences. If you find it, please let me know; I'd like to take a look at it too.

The most original thing you can see is an endless feed of posts in the main content area, preventing you from reaching the footer.

Tip: If you still want to get to it, tap on any post announcement on the homepage and on the page of a specific publication, you'll can do this.

In the case of a WordPress site, all this also works. The main thing is the content and the business it serves. Appearance should help and should not interfere.

Today, this is the picture of the world in the world of web design. Of course, you can see this picture as much more colorful when you use a laptop. You will also use it when looking for a suitable theme for your WordPress site.

When we get to choosing a WordPress theme, I will remind you of this.

17

Does website content matter?

Strange question, isn't it? Of course, content matters.

Have you seen a lot of publications about SEO optimization of texts and the importance of meeting the requirements of search engines?

And you had read the requirements for the texts, you know about backlinks and all that?

And you, apparently, think that you already have some idea about this.

17.1. General information about the content

I have some fresh ideas for you to think about before you get things serious.

1. Content is not only texts. And not even the texts with pictures that are on your site.
2. Your content is not only hosted on your site.
3. Your content is ranked differently by artificial intelligence and search engine algorithms.
4. Your content is rated differently by people.
5. The behavior of your content on the Internet is not always up to you.
6. The behavior of your content on the Internet depends on time and many other factors.
7. If all of the above is understood and considered correctly, then you will get excellent results.

There are many things you need to know and understand about content before you get started.

But it is not very difficult and quite enjoyable.

The topic we discuss deserves, maybe, to write an entire book, but here, we will limit ourselves to just general information that will allow you to understand the most important things about the content.

17.2. Types and forms of content

Usually, when people talk about website content, they mean texts.

Life today has become more complex and diverse. This gives benefits to those who are well-informed.

17.2.1. The content is fundamentally different

We are accustomed in everyday life, when we perceive or transmit information, to deal with texts, photographs, video, and sound.

We still have a sense of smell, touch, and a sense of balance, but Internet technologies have not yet reached them.

Site Content

Text	Images
Body text Headings Excerpts Meta tags	Picture Alt Title Description

Links	Media
Post URL Inbound Outbound Crosslinks	Video Audio Docs Archives

Text is traditionally considered the most important type of content. It is responsible for the meaning of the information, formalizing the whole content and giving it meaning and emotional coloring.

Search engines began to process content from texts, and so far, it plays a crucial role in indexing and classifying sites and determining their place in the overall ranking.

But the development of technologies for processing, indexing, and developing content did not stop there.

Programs can extract captions from images and form text from a soundtrack in a podcast or video. What is written on a photo or heard in a video has a recognizable meaning and is involved in content ranking.

Programs can recognize objects that are shown in photographs and videos. Search engines can find copies of images and select those that are similar to them.

All this is happening and is being done not just for technological development. This is not an end in itself.

The content of the images, the inscriptions on them, and the words that sound in the soundtrack are the same valuable content as the texts.

This content must be produced correctly, too; it will work for your site and bring you traffic.

17.2.2. Content is varied in form

Any content can be short or long. It may or may not contain valuable information.

It may be today attractive to the audience in the form of video and indifferent in the form of text, and tomorrow, the situation may change to the opposite.

Giving content the form in which it will be in demand by the audience is no less necessary than ensuring its fullness of meaning.

Content production issues are somewhat outside the scope of this guide, but we will address them when necessary.

When choosing a form of content, your main task is ensuring it meets the audience's expectations.

Suppose your users come to the site to learn how to make sites that generate income from scratch but find comics about the adventures of a wandering webmaster instead of explanations and instructions. In that case, this will briefly attract their attention.

If your users were drawn in by the promise of watching breathtaking videos on properly riding the world's scariest rides and find a series of boring slideshows instead... well, you get the idea.

The form of content presentation must match the site's content, its purpose, and the audience's expectations.

17.3. Content placement

The modern Internet is designed so that content should be everywhere. Because it is there, everywhere, that your audience is located, and you need to collect it from everywhere on your site, attracting those people who are interested in and need your site.

Be prepared to produce more content than your site can contain and handle. If you work in good faith, there should be no copying. Taking text fragments from publications on the site to post them on social networks is a bad idea. You will do your best if, for each social network, you write text that does not match the texts on the site.

17.3.1. Methods of posting content on the site

There are many ways to place content on the site. Still, the result is always the same: each page of the site that opens when you click on a button, link, image, or menu item and has its address (URL) is considered the central structural unit, the content of which is indexed, ranked, searched and is read.

Content that is crawled, indexed, and counted by various bots is considered relevant to your site:

- words contained in the URL of the page,
- the title of the site or page (title tag, it is worth starting to memorize important words from it),
- the title of the publication, headings, and subheadings of its parts,
- the actual text of the publication,
- text of an excerpt or description of a publication (used by many topics to form feeds of publications on site pages),
- options for SEO titles and descriptions of the publication for search engines and major social networks,
- the texts of the Alt and Description fields for the images contained on the page,
- URLs of the images contained on the page, including the words that make up the filenames,
- texts and addresses of outgoing hyperlinks,
- the images themselves,
- content embedded in the page (videos, fragments, files).

Fortunately, people have learned to represent and use all of the above (and not only) in such a logical way that you will soon learn how to do it, too.

And you will feel quite comfortable.

Note in passing that a URL referring not to the entire page but to a "place" on that page usually ends with the words following the # symbol.

Such addresses are not considered independent, requiring a particular approach.

We will look at this issue in more detail when we discuss the structure of headings and tables of contents (TOC, Table Of Contents).

17.3.2. Ways to post content outside the site

When you remove the splash screen with the "Under Construction" inscription, you start posting your content outside the site and cancel the ban on indexing site pages.

This happens against your will: search robots find your site (if you have provided for it), study its content, and lo and behold, the titles, descriptions, images, and URLs of your site pages can be found in the search results.

Congratulations, you're in business! If, of course, everything is properly taken care of.

And there is something to take care of. If you start posting your content outside the site, you have begun to fight for traffic in this cruel world, where enough people want to get their share even without you. This is a rather uncompromising and fascinating process, so get ready.

A lot of exciting work awaits you:
- regular content updates on the site and notification of search engines about it,
- publications on pages and groups of social networks,
- maintaining pages and chats in messengers,
- own video channels,
- maintenance of thematic feeds in blogs and collective publications,
- writing materials for Q&A services,
- preparing and managing mailing lists,
- posting in forums,
- answers to messages and questions in the comments.

Of course, this is not a complete list. But all the main activities are listed there, each requiring its content.

This is a large and complex job. The reward for it will be the constantly growing traffic to your site and a parallel increase in your income.

18

What does content affect, and how does it do it?

Without a doubt, content determines the fate of the entire project because the content is, generally, is the project.

The site itself, its structure, design, promotion, search positions, and the number of visitors are technologies and results of content delivery and distribution.

Oddly enough, this is often forgotten, and the content is considered simply one of the site's components. This is a mechanistic approach, and it is wrong.

18.1. Content affects the reputation of the site

A website is the primary means of distributing content, a tool. Instead of a website, you could use handwritten paper letters, a series of newspaper articles, or pieces of paper pasted on all the fences and walls of the city.

The results would be different, and the costs - too. But the essence would remain the same.

Fortunately, the Internet makes it possible to do without paper and glue.

At the same time, control over the content distribution process remains entirely in your hands. It is only necessary to understand that this process has long-term and momentary components.

Site reputation is a crucial topic. It is the reputation of the site that determines its fate over long periods.

For the site's reputation to become its visible property, it is necessary to make a lot of effort.

Well-known and influential market participants have come up with various metrics that can be used to evaluate a site's reputation and compare it with competitors.

The names of these metrics are known. The main ones are Page Rank and Domain Authority.

You can find a lot of information about this; we will not waste time here putting it in paraphrasing but rather referring to the originals.

You must understand that these long-term indicators do not develop quickly. They act for a long time but also take a long time to form. The main thing is to ensure that the requirements of search and analytical systems are met from the very beginning and to fulfill them constantly. Then, and only then, will you get the desired result.

The key factors that allow getting high reputation scores are the quality of content and a large amount of traffic.

18.2. Content affects website traffic

It would be possible to call the traffic a "momentary" component of its reputation, influencing the project's fate. This is partly true: traffic is subject to rapid changes, and its fluctuations can be observed in real time.

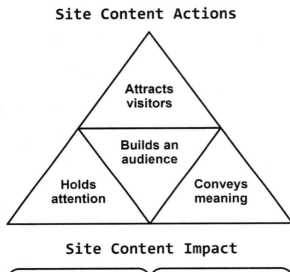

The main feature of traffic as a way to assess the quality of content, a site, and a project as a whole is that traffic is easy to measure and does not require artificially invented indicators. Everything is simple, and we will consider this issue in a separate chapter.

Traffic is also subject to long-term ups and downs.

All fluctuations and changes in traffic are determined solely by how many traffic sources are active at the moment and how many visitors each of them may attract.

There are no other mechanisms.

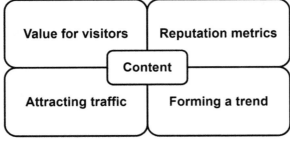

If you start distributing content through another traffic source (social network, bookmarking service, a search engine - the type of source does not matter), then you get traffic from this source.

The amount of traffic from a particular source depends on how many people among the users of this source will see your content and how many of them will want to go to your site to study this content in detail.

Never expect everyone to come to your site to see your links, ads, quotes, banners, or videos. And never be afraid that no one will come.

Don't be surprised if there are suddenly many more or fewer visitors than you expected or than there were yesterday or last week. This is fine. It's just that each traffic source has its management and its own business goals. And they don't always match yours. For now, let's call it that, and in due time, we will consider this issue in detail.

Your only argument is quality content that can attract the target audience you need. It is this argument that is decisive in attracting traffic.

18.3. Content is everything

No search engine, no social network, and no one will ban your site for design (unless you are using outright illegal images or stealing them).

The site's design can be anything if you have no claims of plagiarism or prohibited symbols. This cannot lead to any undesirable consequences.

Your site is also not in danger if it exactly copies the structure of another website or uses similar functions.

Moreover, the structures of similar types of sites are practically the same, and their functionality is the same.

This is how website builders and CMSs work.

But if you copy the content, then you are guaranteed trouble. The nature of these troubles depends on what content you get, where you get it, and where you put it.

A. You took someone else's content (text, image, video, audio) and placed it on your site. Once the author discovers this, you risk losing the site. To begin with, this will be a ban on a domain name and an IP address, but this is just a start. You will only have a domain name that no one will buy from you because of a damaged reputation. If you are using shared hosting, then the innocent sites of your server neighbors will also suffer, and they will have to change hosting (unless, of course, they understand why their traffic suddenly dropped).

B. You've taken someone else's content and posted it to a social network, bookmarking service, creator community site, podcast, or video channel. You run the risk of losing your account and getting banned at the site address that is linked to your account. In some cases, not only your site's domain name can be banned, but also its IP address and even a range of IP addresses for an entire subnet.

C. You have taken your content and reused it on your site. This can also happen unintentionally, for example, when there is an over-reliance on different ways of visual presentation of publications. Search engines may consider such duplication as search spam and lower the site in the search results. Or a case of SEO cannibalism may occur, and the best position in the SERP for a particular one will not be the leading publication you were counting on but another auxiliary material or its presentation. In this case, you may lose views.

D. You've taken your content and posted it to a social network, a bookmarking service, a creator community site, a podcast, or a video channel. For example, you used part of a post posted on the site to announce this post in the feed of a collective online magazine or some outside blog - so that there was simply a link to the original post. In this case, you risk the position of the site in the search results and your account on the external service because many services directly prohibit such a practice.

So follow the simple advice: use only your original content. Today, there are no problems with the production of illustrations or videos. You will spend more time working on the site, but the result is worth it. Borrowing is sometimes perfectly legal and does not harm the site if you know exactly what you are doing.

In some cases, unintentional borrowing is complicated to avoid - for example, if you are writing a textbook or manual, which inevitably contains repeated common truths that cannot be avoided without losing the integrity and coherence of the entire material.

You will learn more about the importance of unique content from publications dedicated to website promotion.

19

What is
the importance
of website speed?

The speed of your website is as essential as the quality of the content you publish. The attitude towards it, both on the part of visitors, search engines, and other significant traffic sources, depends on the website's work speed.

19.1. Site speed and search engines

There are many search engines in the world. The permanent leader of this segment - the Google search engine - is the primary source of search traffic, but its less noticeable competitors should not be discounted.

You can never accurately predict which search engine will bring a new client, buyer, or interested reader to your site. Therefore, you need to work with all search engines. Search engine robots will evaluate your site according to different criteria. Speed is one of them.

Some search engines only measure how fast your site gives a response to a query sent to it. Others may also measure page load time. The more advanced ones, like Google, measure various metrics, with your website speed data taking center stage (we'll cover this in more detail in the Core Web Vitals metrics chapter).

Why do search engines do this? They just get ahead of the future of your site (and pretty much define it).

Search engines have accumulated gigantic statistics. The Google search engine, which is integrated with the Google Analytics statistics analysis system, has data on the relationship between the speed of sites and their visitors' behavior.

Naturally, the desire to increase their efficiency leads to the fact that search engines, when generating results for specific search queries, prioritize sites with higher performance ratings. If your website has the same quality content as your competitor's website but is slower, then your competitor's website will appear higher in the search feed.

If the search engine algorithms consider that the pages of your site are so slow that it does not meet their technical requirements, then the positions of these pages can drop significantly. These pages may even be wholly excluded from the search!

In general, website speed is critical to successfully driving search traffic.

19.2. Site speed and other sources of traffic

Social networks, bookmarking services, catalogs, and directories are not very demanding on the speed of sites. For them, the most important thing is the content.

By content, in this case, we mean not only the content of the site itself but also the content of various fields of additional methods of internal markup of your site's pages.

Site Speed

```
┌─ Data ──────────────────────┐
│                             │
│    • Server Response Speed  │
│       • Page Loading Time   │
│    • Page Full-Drawing Time │
│    • Page interaction speed │
│    • Speed on Slow Devices  │
│       • Core Web Vitals     │
└─────────────────────────────┘
```

```
┌─ Impact ────────────────────┐
│                             │
│  • Getting Search Traffic   │
│  • Driving Social Traffic   │
│    • Retaining Visitors     │
│    • Improving Authority    │
│       • Raising Ranking     │
└─────────────────────────────┘
```

Difficult? Don't worry; we'll take a look at that in due course.

For now, just keep in mind that it's unlikely that other traffic sources will mistreat your site because of its slow speed.

Although even if it is incredibly slow, the algorithms of such systems may consider this a sign that your site is not working at all. But this is almost impossible if you can normally open its pages on your computer using a browser.

Most likely, even if they do not open very quickly (for example, because of the beautiful effects you diligently set up and attractive backgrounds you are very proud of), you can take it easy. But this does not mean visitors who found your site in a search engine or went to its page from a social network will react similarly.

19.3. Website speed and its visitors

You can see from your own experience that modern visitors are very capricious.

Of course, suppose you publish unique content on your site that is incredibly exciting and useful or sell something vital and unsurpassed in quality. In that case, the visitor will wait for the page he opened to load fully.

But life is such that you most likely have a lot of competitors. They try very hard to get ahead of each other and you. Therefore, their sites are also well-made and work very quickly. This means that your site should also work very fast. Even faster than competitors. Presently, the limits of the patience of a user who surfs the Internet or searches for the information he needs on sites are quite accurately defined. Companies estimate these limits differently, but we will try to average them.

It can be considered that the full loading time of the page after clicking on the link or after entering the address in the browser should not exceed 1.5 - 2 seconds. The same rule applies to user actions that involve reloading the page, for example, when scrolling through a product catalog.

If your site responds to user actions more slowly, the user will likely leave your site and go to competitors. When you operate your site, you can obtain pretty accurate information about user behavior using Google Analytics or similar. For now, remember that speed is critical to retaining visitors.

20

What is website traffic, and why is it so important?

It may seem strange to many web admins and Internet users, but most people do not know what website traffic is. Maybe you did not think about this because your thoughts were occupied with your profession, which is far from this topic.

At the same time, even the most distant people from this topic naturally understand that visitors should come to the site. Otherwise, the site will be useless.

20.1. History of the traffic question

In times immemorial, when the primary traffic source was the visitors themselves, each site had a button on all pages to add its address to the browser bookmarks.

Now, the vast majority of sites do not have it because it has come to be considered archaic and useless. It is replaced by buttons for social networks, bookmarking services, and instant messengers.

Website visitors spend more of their lives on the Internet than ever. Therefore, they have many more opportunities to save and share information. They stopped remembering site addresses and storing them only in browser bookmarks.

Capturing a user's attention (even a very interested in your content), getting him to go to the site, remembering the site address, and becoming a regular visitor has become much more complicated than before.

Of the traditional methods of "preserving" the audience, perhaps only work with mailing lists by e-mail has been preserved. But this method is only suitable for working with users you attracted to your site earlier. The number of subscribers by itself can only decrease, not increase. Accordingly, each subsequent mailing will give, on average, fewer visits to the site than the previous one.

But we digress a little.

The second traditional source of traffic has historically been directories and site directories.

Almost none of them survived. The "Yellow Pages" and "White Pages" have gone down in history, even on paper. On the Internet, their fate was, to be honest, sealed from the very beginning.

Search engines have become the third traditional source of traffic. They not only survived but also occupied the main positions in this capacity. You need to understand that traffic from other traffic sources for your site may also depend on major search engines.

To simplify the further presentation, we will focus primarily on search engines.

20.2. What is traffic actually?

If you think traffic is the number of visitors coming to your site, for example, within a day or a whole month, then you are undoubtedly right.

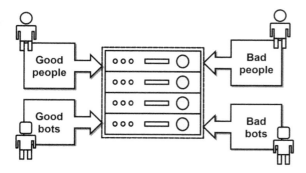

But this is just the tip of the iceberg called the "mountain of traffic information."

Each of your visitors can be "targeted," "interested," or "random." He may visit your site for the first time or return to it daily, once a week, or five times a year.

If you think that these details are not so important, then you are mistaken. Important. And not only these details but much more.

Let's consider some fundamental indicators for some abstract periods related to traffic, but so far, not in great detail. We will view them from the positions of the search engine.

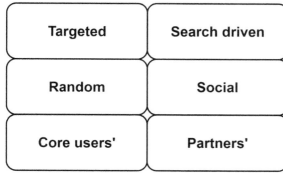

The number of visitors is the number of unique IP addresses of computers and mobile devices on which pages of your site were loaded (this can be real people, useful search engine bots, useless statistics gathering bots for other people's interests, or malicious bots).

The percentage of new visitors. The higher it is, the more attractive the page's content is for the audience and vice versa.

The percentage of previous visitors who return to your site. The higher it is, the more valuable your content is for the audience.

The average number of page loads per visitor. The download may not be counted if the visitor spent little time on the page. The more pages per session, on average, viewed by each site visitor, the better your site.

Average time on page. The smaller it is, the more useless the page's content will be considered.

The number of interactions on the page (swiping, clicking buttons, filling out forms, expanding lists, browsing galleries, and everything else like that). The larger it is, the more engaging and well-organized the page's content will be considered.

Percentage of visitors who left the site after viewing only the page they opened via a link from the SERP (Search Engine Results Page). The higher it is, the less attractive your site is for them, and the worse the structure of its content is organized.

The percentage of visitors who visited another page on your site after viewing the previous one. The higher it is, the more attractive your site is to them, and the better its content structure is.

For starters, you should probably stop. You have already understood that traffic is not such a primitive thing.

For it to be "quality," you will need to attract the exact people potentially interested in your site and give them the well-structured information they need so much in their lives. Everything is very simple, right?

20.3. Why and for what is traffic important?

The answer to this question is obvious, and you have known it for a long time: Website traffic is necessary for the success of your entire project.

Suppose you remember the two previous paragraphs of this chapter.

In that case, this will be supplemented by the understanding that traffic, or rather, its particular indicators' values, is essential for search engines. These values allow search engines to give pages on your site the positions in search results that search engines think they deserve.

The higher the positions of your site pages in the search engine results, the more traffic will be on your site, and the better it will be.

The more traffic on your site and the better it is, the higher the positions of your site pages in the search engine results will be.

Is the circle closed?

In general, yes.

Also, keep in mind the following.

How much traffic your site receives will be known to the whole world.

Special services with varying degrees of accuracy and different methods will evaluate all its characteristics and enter the information into their databases.

This information will be used to build your site's dossier, including Domain Authority, Page Rank, and more.

Both your competitors and your competitors' competitors will have access to your website dossier. This dossier will be available to various services, networks, government, and commercial services that provide data to multiple users.

Take care of traffic and its quality from the very beginning. We will repeatedly return to this topic when discussing the site's design, creation, and operation.

You will have the opportunity not to miss any essential thoughts related to the site's traffic issues.

21

Preliminary SEO project for your future website

What is SEO, what is behind this acronym, and how to achieve success in it? Why is everyone talking about SEO? Why is SEO important, and what does it have to do with a website project?

21.1. What is SEO really?

SEO (Search Engine Optimisation) is defined as improving the quality and increasing the amount of free traffic that goes to a website or its page from search engines.

Sounds good, right? Improving quality is good, and increasing traffic volume is also good. And besides, it's free!

It would seem that this is not difficult. After all, everyone does this, and all the technologies have long been known. It is necessary to create a website and do, in the end, this SEO to get a lot of quality traffic from search engines for free.

Do what? Take detailed instructions and arrange keywords by site pages? Implement micro-markup? Buy a lot of external links? Hire an SEO man to do it all the way it should be done?

If you think something like this, you are most likely planning a failed project.

The fact is that the generally accepted definition of SEO has the so-called phenomenological character. It's not even a definition; it's a description.

No wonder this definition describes SEO as a "process" without revealing its essence.

Such a superficial understanding of SEO is not far from the "cargo cult." This often happens: there are a lot of external links, all the requirements of specialists are met, and nothing is forgotten.

Everything is done! The site owner is waiting for the result, but there is none. There is not enough traffic, or the wrong people come.

What's the reason?

What's done wrong if it's done right?

It's just that all the work is built on the phenomenological definition of SEO. And that job is to ensure that your content reaches the audience with minimal obstacles and losses.

As soon as you understand that this was not enough and formulate the problem, then, most likely, yourself or, with the help of a specialist, will conclude that you have incorrectly or insufficiently qualitatively formed the semantic core (we will talk about it later).

If you perfectly redo the semantic core and repeat the long, time-consuming, and expensive SEO optimization process but again do not achieve the desired result, in that case, you have only your cargo cult improved.

Don't do this.

Don't even start until you know precisely why. Now I will help you solve this once and for all.

What is SEO

 SEO IS MARKETING

SEO starts
before the idea of the project.

Bad SEO
You want people to search
for the content you create.

Good SEO
 You create content that
people are searching for.

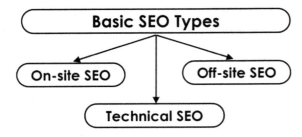

Basic SEO Types

On-site SEO   **Off-site SEO**

Technical SEO

When someone talks about search engine optimization, they mean or claim something like "the user enters a search query, and you need the pages of your site to be as high as possible in the SERP feed."

That's not the whole truth.

Before typing words in the search bar, the user has already "typed" them in his head.

Genuine search engine optimization is just the situation when what is "typed" in the head of the user can be found on your site.

You will say that this is no longer SEO but marketing. And you'd be right.

Because SEO is, actually, the small, and not the most complicated, part of marketing.

21.2. SEO is, firstly, marketing

If we discuss SEO as a part of marketing, we don't need to develop a new interpretation, such as "selection expression optimization." What we already have, we are pretty satisfied with.

We'll do it easier. Let's see what marketers can tell us.

Marketing professionals know three things very well (actually much more):

- marketing begins at the moment when the first thought about a future product appears in someone's head,
- bad marketing is when you try to sell what you can produce just because you can't produce something else,
- good marketing is when you produce something you can sell because people need it.

Let's skip all the intermediate arguments for brevity; they are reasonably obvious.

The first thought leads us to the conclusion that you need to start taking care of SEO from the first minute you have an idea for a future project.

The second thought leads us to conclude that if no one is interested in the project and nobody will nowhen look for it (or don't look for it right now), doing SEO is a waste of time and money.

The third thought leads us to conclude that if a project is attractive to people and they will look for it and find it, then good SEO can significantly help the project, and bad SEO will not be able to destroy it.

All you need is to develop a project that will interest the target audience (another subject for consideration in a separate post) and then make the proper positioning, description, and content.

The first part of the sentence you just read outlines the true essence of SEO, and we just talked about it.

The second part of the sentence concerns the mistakes that should not be made. What exactly should not be wrong? We will now talk about this briefly and consider each aspect of SEO in more detail in separate chapters.

Let's sum it up.

SEO begins when you have formulated an idea for a future project.

Bad SEO is when you try to promote the content you've managed to create.

Good SEO is when you make content that people want to find.

21.3. SEO is, secondly, everything else

Here, we're going to talk about what everyone calls SEO.

Once you've determined who your user is and what exactly they will search for (and find) on your site, you will begin a real SEO job for the start phase of creating your website.

Here, we will give a shortlist and then consider all its positions in separate publications.

Once you have formulated the idea and content of your project, you need to do the following (remember I told you that you would need a checkered notebook?):

- write down the name of your project as it will be indicated on the site and how it will be displayed in the search results (with a line length of up to 50 characters, everyone will see it in full, and everyone will be able to read it, up to 60 characters - 90% of users, and more than 60 characters it not recommended),

- write down a description of your project for the same purposes; you need to focus on the minimum length of 50 characters and the maximum length of 150 characters (in extreme cases, 160).

The title and description of the project should contain as few meaningless words and prepositions as possible.

The beginnings of the title and description should start with the most important words expressing the idea of the project.

What you just wrote down in your notebook will be your starting point.

Remember the chapter about the different types of content and how to put it on the site?

It's time to start using your knowledge.

1. Write the first version of the content plan (draft). It should contain the site categories' names and descriptions, titles - and briefs - for the posts. Don't miss it! This stage is critical; work conscientiously and do not miss anything.

2. Separately write down the key phrase (keyword combination, keywords) for each category and each post. This will become the basis of the semantic core in the

future (there will be a separate chapter about it).

3. Create a list of illustrations as you see them at this stage. For each illustration, write down its title in the form in which it will be used in the name of the file (and in the URL of the image on the site) and the name in the form in which it will be displayed on the site (from 5 to 9 words), and the description (no more than 250 characters).

Here's why you'll need it:

- to identify the most important keywords that you can use when registering a domain name,
- to form the semantic core of your site,
- for use in the preparation of future posts for publication and indexing,
- for the preparation of off-site publications (off-site SEO).

What will remain in your notebook is the foundation of your future well-being!

22

Technical SEO
of your website

Technical SEO is all ways to improve your website's interaction with the outside world that don't directly relate to the content.

22.1. How does your site appear to the world?

22.1.1. Access protocol: HTTP or HTTPS, and what is the SSL certificate

Your site starts with a domain name; we have already discussed this.

To access your site by its domain name, users (and search engines) must use an address that includes the domain name and the access protocol.

If the site uses the HTTP access protocol, you are in trouble.

Search engines won't take your site seriously - they will mark its pages as "not good enough" and never give it a high position in the search.

Browsers will mark pages on your site as "not secure enough" when loading pages on your site, and visitors will see this.

All social networks, bookmarking services, and thematic communities - everyone will know about it.

In addition, your competitors know this, too, so they have already purchased SSL certificates and switched their sites to the HTTPS protocol. You can't do without it either.

We will discuss the types of SSL certificates, which of them suits you best, and how to connect it in a separate chapter.

Another important note about addressing a site using various protocols is in the chapter you will read now.

22.1.2. Site address options with *www* and without *www*

If the site has a domain name *allthebestintheworld.com*, then after placing the website with the hoster and binding the domain name to it, the site will be available at the addresses "*allthebestintheworld.com*" and "*www.allthebestintheworld.com*."

This is usually because the hoster does not know your intentions in advance. In the configuration of DNS records, the versions of the addresses with *www* and without *www* are described as synonyms, that is, equal addresses for accessing the site.

It would seem that this is ok. It's such a tradition, and all sites have it.

It's not like that at the same time.

Yes, this is a tradition; it was not without meaning, and now it is, too. It's just that most sites aren't sophisticated enough to have versions other than *www*, i.e., a universal web version based on classic HTML. But that doesn't mean that different versions don't or can't exist. Now, we will leave the question of other versions aside; we are not interested in them yet.

Technical SEO

```
┌─ Project ──────────────────────────────────┐
│  Domain Name & Thematic Niche & Semantic Core &    │
│  Content Plan & Site Structure & Site Functionality │
│  & Site Design & Users Behaviour & Users Experience │
└────────────────────────────────────────────┘

┌─ Speed ────────────────────────────────────┐
│  Server Location & Ping Speed & Server Power &      │
│  Server Resources & CMS Speed & Site Optimization & │
│  Server Cache & Browser Cache & CDN Services        │
└────────────────────────────────────────────┘

┌─ Crawling ─────────────────────────────────┐
│  Content Hierarchy & Sitemap Files &        │
│  robots.txt File & URL Structure & BreadCrumbs &    │
│  Site Pagination & Content Actuality &      │
│  No Broken Links & Indexing Bots Access     │
└────────────────────────────────────────────┘

┌─ Indexing ─────────────────────────────────┐
│  Using Search Console & No Duplicated Content &     │
│  SSL & Correct Redirects & Responsive Pages &       │
│  No HTTP Errors & Structured Data Schemes   │
│  & Mobile Friendly & IndexNow Tool          │
└────────────────────────────────────────────┘
```

The fact is that the equality of addresses with *www* and without *www* (since there are versions other than *www*, as we just mentioned) is regarded by search services as the existence of two duplicate versions of the site pages accessible under these different addresses.

Do you understand what the trick is? Most users believe that addresses with and without *www* are the same thing, but search engines do not agree with this statement.

Search engines regard this situation as the presence of two duplicate versions of the site with the same content but with different page addresses.

This is a direct path to trouble because there is no greater sin, according to search bots, search algorithms, and search engines, than trying to get them to index duplicate content.

In the previous chapter, we discussed accessing the site via various protocols - the unsecured HTTP and secure HTTPS protocols.

Have you already purchased an SSL certificate and connected access via HTTPS protocol?

If you have not followed the correct steps to configure the addressing of your site, then the whole world, including search engines, will know that your site does not even have 2 but 4 duplicate versions available at different addresses:

http://allthebestintheworld.com
http://www.allthebestintheworld.com
https://allthebestintheworld.com
https://www.allthebestintheworld.com

Of course, you already guessed this should not be the case.

In this regard, your task is to inform search engines that there are no duplicate versions, that there is only one version available at the address *https://allthebestintheworld.com*, and all other addresses simply lead to the same version of the site.

This is not difficult to do, and we will consider this issue in a separate chapter in the Build Site category. Now, you must only understand why this is necessary.

22.2. How your website interacts with visitors

We consider here everyone as visitors - fans and competitors of your project, search engine bots, other useful bots, useless bots, and malicious bots.

We will still talk about how to deal with useless and malicious bots in publications about security.

Now, our task is to give to usual users and useful bots what they want the way they want.

They want content quickly and without errors.

If you do everything right and build your site as I teach you, then there will be no mistakes, and everything will work correctly and exactly as users expect.

As for the speed of its operation, this critical part of the requirements is not under our full control. But it is extremely critically perceived by the whole surrounding world, as we have already discussed.

With knowledge, we can minimize the risks of meeting these requirements and restrictions. Here's what you need to know.

22.2.1. The speed of the hosting

A fairly high speed of the server and communication channels can be obtained, even if you use cheap shared hosting.

This is unsurprising if you have placed your site on a modern, high-quality hosting platform.

Problems, in this case, will begin when you have a large number of neighbors on the server, and they buy or somehow attract a large amount of traffic, place a lot of "heavy" information, or connect complex solutions to their sites that require large computing resources.

At an unpredictable moment, the response speed and processing speed of requests on your hosting may decrease, and this will not depend on you. If, at this time, your site decides to visit the search engine robot, then it will fix low-speed indicators, and this will have a bad effect on the positions of the pages of your site in search.

How critical is that? Of course, this depends on how much traffic you get and intend to receive from search engines.

But it is better to avoid this.

How to do this - we will discuss it later. For now, just lock it into your memory; it's important.

22.2.2. Website speed

Even on fast hosting, your website may not be fast enough.

We will now list the main reasons and will not consider them in detail. In the future, we'll cover them in detail.

Here are the possible leading causes:
- too heavy and slow WordPress theme is installed;
- too many plugins are installed;

- too complex and heavy plugins are used;
- too many visual effects;
- too large images are used;
- images are used, the size and proportions of which are not optimal;
- third-party codes that slow down the work have been used;
- missing or poorly configured caching plugin;
- browser-side caching is missing or poorly configured.
- various codes and resources that are not needed are loaded on the site's pages.

Too extensive a list? Do not be afraid. As you move forward, you will see that there is nothing mysterious about each of its points.

22.3. What is important to understand

Correctly done work on the technical part of SEO, as you can see from the text of this post, is very important.

However, it is not related to the content of the site. It's that simple.

If you do all the technical SEO work correctly and efficiently, you will eliminate many obstacles you may encounter.

Technical SEO won't make your website a winner automatically. But if you don't do the technical SEO work, your website will inevitably be among the losers.

Technical SEO is a necessary part of the job, but it's not enough. It is not enough to have a perfectly acting website; you also need it to contain everything you need to solve the problems of your business and do it well.

This is called "on-site SEO".

23

On-site SEO:
How is it done?

On-site SEO is precisely that part of the job, often referred to simply as SEO. This is part of the SEO job that is entirely up to you and that you can have complete control over.

As we have already said, this part of the work begins with the first steps to create the future project, with its name, description, and domain name.

Your website should be a well-structured collection of different types of content. The site's content should be structured and presented to make visitors convenient. The site's content should be structured and described to be understandable to search engines.

23.1. Structuring content on the site

The structure of any site is predetermined by the following:
- internal semantic connections of the content,
- the required logic of the interaction of the site visitor with the content,
- technical capabilities of content structuring.

23.1.1. Semantic and logical connections of content on the site

You determine the internal semantic connections of the content blocks with each other as the site's author.

This should be done by considering the targets, methods, and technologies used to attract visitors to the site.

For example, if a visitor comes to the landing page, he is eventually required to fill out a registration form and leave his address or phone number in the site database.

In this case, the logic of interaction with the content is elementary - the visitor moves around the page linearly, and your task is to sufficiently warm up his interest by the time he reaches the registration form.

The rest of the site's content has an auxiliary value and may even be completely absent.

If a visitor is to get to an arbitrary publication (for example, from search results), then he should be able to find out which category this publication belongs to, what tags it is associated with, what was published before it, and what - after it.

That is, the visitor should be able to navigate "on which page he opened the book" and go to the place he needs.

Suppose your site contains content diverse in form and purpose (news, galleries, articles, surveys, tests, or something else). In that case, the user should quickly navigate this diversity and visually choose what interests him.

Publications should also have a prominent structure, including properly written internal headings, numbered and bulleted lists, and internal and external links.

At the design stage of the site, your imagination in organizing the content of the future site will have no limits.

You will have to limit it forcibly so the development process does not get out of control.

Technical requirements for the structure of the content perfectly cope with this.

23.1.2. Technical structuring of content on the site

The hierarchical principle of structuring content is predetermined by the fact that any site has a "top" - a home page addressed by a domain name. Below this peak is everything that is on the site.

Even if only one category exists on the site, we will get a two-level hierarchical model.

To organize the content, the following main types of taxonomies are available to us:

- categories (can be nested),
- tags (cannot be nested).

These taxonomies form a system of logical relationships between publications.

There are also additional types of taxonomies that are considered "hidden." To be precise, they are simply auxiliary and are not independent. These include various publication formats and a menu system.

Publication formats only affect the presentation of post content.

A menu system is simply a visual representation of category links.

On-Site SEO

> Texts

Post Title & Post Description & Post Excerpts &
Post Keywords & Text Length & Headings &
Last Modified Date & Internal Links
& Outbound Links

> Media

File Format & File Size & File Name with Keywords
& Alt Field & Title Field & Caption Field &
Description Field & Featured Images
& Images in Post & Lazy Loading

> Meta

Meta Title & Meta Description &
OG Social Meta Tags &
Twitter Social Meta Tags & Meta Robots

> Schemes

Logo and Publisher & WebSite & Article & Video &
FAQ & Local Business & How To & Recipe & Course &...

The structure of the links in the menu may or may not coincide with the actual structure of the categories, but we noted this only to emphasize their secondary nature.

WordPress allows you to create your taxonomies if necessary, but this is still beyond our needs.

23.2. Presentation of content on the site

23.2.1. Keywords

When it comes to SEO, you need to follow a few simple rules.

1. Search engines analyze the content of the site pages without missing any details. This means that keywords must be used in the correct form and the right quantities in many places – from the names of menu items to the content of alt fields for images.
2. Keywords should be present in sufficient, but not excessive, quantity.
3. Keywords should correspond to the subject of the publication.

We will consider this topic in more detail in the future.

23.2.2. Visual representation

You may not be aware of this, but search engines analyze some things that may seem secondary.

But their impact on a site's position in the SERPs can change your mind.

1. The size of the buttons or links that can be clicked and the distance between them in height and width - matter. The search bot will notice buttons that are too small and letters that are too close to each other.
2. If you decide for design reasons to depict some inscriptions in a delicate purple color on a pale pink background (shades are not essential; the principle is important), then for insufficiently contrasting text, expect punishment, too.
3. Images must have a suitable size and correctly filled service fields.
4. The entire text of the publication should be easy to read.

We don't continue this list yet. But you get the idea, right? The site pages should not be as likely pleasant to the eye pictures. They should be easy to perceive and interact with. Search engines know how to evaluate this.

23.3. Internal markup of content

The site's content has properties that are not visible to the visitor but are visible and necessary for various valuable instruments, such as social media tools.

23.3.1. Required and optional fields, tags, and parameters

If you want to share the site's publications on social networks successfully, you must use particular types of internal markup.

The most common of these are known as Facebook OpenGraph and Twitter Cards.

If these markups aren't embedded in your site's page codes, you must manually enter the address, title, description, and illustration each time you share your post.

There are also mandatory fields that can be found only when you look at the codes of the pages of the site. These are fields with the title of the page, its description, language indication, and others.

Without these fields, your website, from the point of view of search engines, does not exist.

23.3.2. Micro-markup schemes

Structured Data Markup Types, also known as Structured Data or Schemes, is a specific standard and technology for describing data on a website page.

This technology is designed to provide search engine robots with accurate information about the nature and properties of the page's content.

Here are examples of such schemes: article, recipe, course, program, book, F.A.Q., how-to, and others.

Using such markup technology can provide advantages in indexing. If search engine robots detect such markup on pages, these pages are considered "improved." Of course, this is important.

23.4. How to deal with on-site SEO challenges

We have not covered the issues of providing on-site SEO in great detail, but this volume of information is enough to puzzle an inexperienced person.

Do not be afraid of the diversity and number of tasks. A considerable amount of experience has been accumulated to solve them, which can be used without problems.

You must follow simple rules and use the right plugins to solve SEO problems.

We will discuss these issues in more detail later.

24

Off-site SEO:
how is it done?

Off-site SEO needs to be taken literally. This is all the work related to promoting your site, which is done outside the website, and there is much of such work.

We will consider here only the main directions of this work. When discussing off-site SEO, they usually forget to start with the most important thing. It's odd, but it's true.

We will not repeat this mistake. We don't give details here yet. We'll talk more about them ahead.

24.1. The main, very first steps in off-site SEO

After all, it is so obvious: you need to establish the right connections between your website and the search engines for which SEO is done.

1. To do this, you must create two files that your site does not need but are necessary for search engines and put these files in your site's root directory. You may have heard of these files. These are robots.txt and sitemaps.xml.
2. You need to register in special search engine services designed for web admins that allow you to control the situation.
3. You need to link your websites and search console services. To do this, you must add site addresses to your account and confirm your rights to them.

There are additional operations and opportunities, and we will consider them separately.

24.2. External links are what everyone is talking about

The situation in SEO is such that external links that lead to the pages of your website are considered the essential thing in off-site SEO. A complete list of such links is usually called the site's link profile. The more links, the better: your website is considered in-demand and exciting, and visitors actively retain links to its pages wherever they can.

Search engines carefully track the links that lead to your site and decide which ones are good and which are bad.

Many "good links" mean that your site is good and can be raised in the SERPs. A lot of "bad links" mean that the site is also "bad" and can be omitted in the SERPs.

The more links, the better: your website is considered in-demand and exciting, and visitors actively retain links to its pages wherever they can. Since this approach to external links has existed for a long time, there are a lot of contradictions here.

Off-Site SEO

Information Environment Research

Search Trends

Competitors' SEO

Keywords Stats

Competitors Ranking

Attracting and growing the audience

Email Subscribers

Messengers

Social Media

Mobile Apps, PWA

Increasing Reach and Traffic

Link Building

Guest Posts

Video and Podcasts

Email Marketing

Forums and QA Services

Bookmarking

Representatives of search engines also regularly make contradictory statements. They may suddenly inform the world that external links no longer matter, but in the tools of the webmaster console, they save a section with statistics about such links.

SEO specialists also behave in contradiction.

However, no one undertakes to argue that the site may not have any link profile. External links are needed. Otherwise, how will the whole world know about your website?

Around the construction of the "link profile," many services, agencies, exchanges, and other handy resources were created. Only "good" ones that give "good links" should be used. Do you know where to look for them? Various analytical, consulting, and reference services are ready to provide you with assistance in finding them.

Many tricks, ways, and technologies exist for building external links profiles. We will not try to compete with specialists on these issues; we have entirely different tasks now. But the basic information about this you will get.

For now, record this task in your workbook.

24.3. Incoming traffic is what it's all about

Of course, that's right. What else do you need for your business if the website is already ready?

The site itself and external links are the basis for proper interaction with search engines. Search engines are the source of traffic. If done correctly, the site will have stable traffic from search engines, and all you have to do is run your business calmly and pay taxes, right?

No, that's not all true.

Firstly, if your site is in good standing with search engines and its pages fall into the most advanced positions of the search results, then this is not forever. Competitors are doing everything they can to throw you off the podium. Search engines regularly redo their algorithms, naturally, in their favor. The market is changing, information is becoming obsolete, and new sites are emerging. You will have to make efforts to keep the occupied positions in the search results.

Secondly, traffic from search engines is good, but there are other traffic sources as well. You cannot do without social networks, bookmarking, forums, and Q&A services. Moreover, these sources can give many times more traffic than search engines.

Thirdly, it is not enough to get external traffic in sufficient quantities to have high-quality content, know your product well, and believe in yourself. You need to know what's happening in your market segment, how your competitors feel, and where they're getting traffic from.

24.4. Analysis of competitors' websites

Just keep in mind that you can't do without it.

It would be best to research your market segment thoroughly; this work should be regular.

Before launching the project, you will need to understand what is happening in your market segment during the launch - make the necessary adjustments after launch - control the dynamics of changes in the position of your site, and make efforts to improve it.

Many SEO experts recommend starting work on the project with the analysis of competitors. Everyone always does that in real life (not on the Internet), right?

We will further consider the work of analyzing competitors' sites in more detail.

24.5. Conclusion

You've read the latest chapter from an introductory series of lessons about website content and the main types of SEO.

For the knowledge you have gained to become closer to practical application, we will talk in the next chapter about the site's semantic core.

25

Working with
the site's semantic core

The semantic core does not have a generally accepted definition since this term can have different interpretations depending on the context.
We will discuss all aspects related to the semantic core.

25.1. The semantic core is a phrasebook for specialists in your market segment

Definition: The semantic core is all the words and phrases that describe your product, your services, your activities, and the content of your website.

Simply put, the semantic core characterizes the professional lexicon, professional terminology, professional activity, and how the client or buyer sees all this.

It's not very difficult to understand. If you are well versed in your profession and know your subject area, you can easily collect all of the above, for example, in one text file.

What to do with such a file, and why is it needed?

All this "phrasebook" should form the basis of your website and describe its values and meaning.

Don't make the usual mistake! Always start scraping the semantic core with your own knowledge and insights, not by analyzing your audience's search queries.

You need to know precisely - what you know and how you will dispose of your knowledge. This is the basis, and all the following stages serve to strengthen and develop it but cannot replace it.

25.2. The semantic core is the semantic skeleton of the website

Definition: The semantic core is all the words and phrases that should be contained in the titles, descriptions, and primary and auxiliary fields of your site's content.

During the design phase of the site, you can assemble a semantic core in the form of a spreadsheet, a structured list, or another form convenient for you.

To prevent this work from turning into mechanical sorting, I recommend that you go through the hierarchy of taxonomies of the site on a top-down basis.

The name of the site and its description should contain a precisely formulated general idea of the site. If this is a workshop site for making buckles for dog collars, call it that. If the site allows you to sell products - add the word "store" to the name. But have you forgotten that you have to keep within 50-60 characters? And in the description - no more than 150?

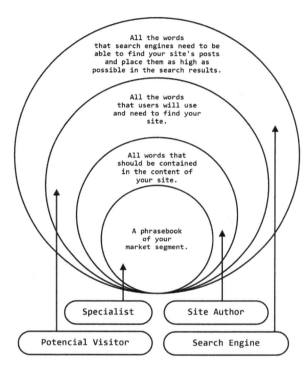

Semantic Core

Four Points of View

In the names of the next level of the taxonomy hierarchy - categories - there should be other specific keywords (we first used this term when describing the semantic core, right?), their own for each category, narrower in meaning (diamond buckles, just gold buckles, buckles with digital lock, etc.).

In the titles and content of posts, even narrower keywords should be used. This is very similar to the pattern, the parts of which do not repeat each other.

Your task is to build such a hierarchy of keywords and phrases that it includes everything that makes up your professional dictionary, and at the same time, as in an actual dictionary, its separate parts do not repeat each other.

But unlike a regular dictionary, in which words are grouped by letters of the alphabet, and each letter corresponds to their simple linear list, you should get a hierarchical structure in which the lexicon will be grouped by meaning and ordered within groups according to the intended behavior of the user or the desired development of the plot.

Essentially, you should get a ready-made skeleton of the site, which will just need to be filled with content, observing the rules of content creation. In part, we have already considered these rules.

25.3. The semantic core is what is created for searching

Definition: The semantic core is all the words and phrases that need to be discovered, indexed, ranked, and used by search engines to determine the purpose of your website and its place in the SERPs.

Once upon a time, search engines used only the title, description, and keyword fields to understand the content of pages.

Then, the analysis of all the content was added, and the search became known as full-text.

Subsequently, the keywords field became optional, and search engine algorithms learned to make an idea about the meaning of the site content, its authenticity, naturalness, uniqueness, and other essential characteristics. This allowed all of us to avoid abuse (such as search junk) and increase the quality of texts.

But the semantic guideline in any text for search engines is still keywords. Therefore, you need to be able to work with them correctly so that the pages of your site appear in the search results in those places that correspond to them.

25.4. The semantic core is what the user wants

Definition: The semantic core is all the words and phrases by which users will try to find your site.

Of course, this is not entirely true, or even not at all. Users will not try to access your site. They will try to find the first site that comes across, which will be at the top of the search results for specific keywords, and some reason will cause a desire to go to it.

But the essence of the matter does not change from this.

The importance of the user's interests is most often put in the first place when it comes to the formation of the semantic core.

SEOs who have no idea about dog buckles or any other area of activity other than SEO are thus making their lives easier.

They are right in their way: to discover visitors' interests, there is absolutely no need to delve into your professional secrets and subtleties.

But this does not exempt you from the need to do your part of the work conscientiously: prepare the site's content! After all, everything is decided by the content, and no SEO specialist can create it for you.

An SEO specialist (or yourself, if you have the time and patience) can refine the composition of the semantic core for you based on actual search query statistics.

25.5. Conclusion

We discussed the concept of the site's semantic core, and now you can look at it from different angles.

It's practical and beneficial.

You now have more information to think about the structure and content of your future website.

In addition, you now know what a semantic core is and why you need it. Not only can you keep up a conversation on this topic, but also quite consciously set tasks for yourself, your business partners, and SEO specialists.

26

Website front end:
what is it

The front end is a term that has become popular in recent times. Front end development is now a separate profession. Why is all this happening?

26.1. How we see the front end of the site

We deliberately do not give, for now, a definition of the front end so that it becomes clear a little later.

From the discussed name itself, it is clear that we are talking about that part of the website that is facing somewhere "forward."

"Forward," in this case, should be understood as the part of the site facing its visitor. That is its visible part.

The same part with which the site displays its content and interacts with the visitor. The same part of the website that we used to call pages, posts, categories, forms, directories, and other familiar words.

It is clear that the front end does not exist by itself, and a browser is needed to display and interact with it.

Undoubtedly, many of you have encountered a situation where the same sites or individual pages are displayed differently and work differently in different browsers and devices.

Such cases indicate that the site's front end is either poorly implemented technically or deliberately (which happens much less often), causing visitors to use specific devices and browsers.

Front-end compatibility with different browsers and devices is critical when developing a website. Any compatibility issues inevitably lead to the loss of part of the audience.

So, the front end is what we see in the browser window, and at the same time, what we see may differ in different browsers and on different types of devices.

26.2. What exactly do we see as a front end?

We see in the browser window, of course, not the front end itself but the results of its interaction with the browser.

Since all browsers are developed differently, they usually display the site's pages differently, too.

It does not make sense to consider this topic in detail here; it is enough to fix this fact so that in the hereafter, the differences in the display and behavior of pages on different devices will not cause you surprise or fear.

As you study the subject of building websites, you will have a sufficient understanding. It's time to clarify what we mean by "different browsers" and "different devices" here.

Since you know how to use a computer, you probably already know the following things:

- applications that work on one computer may not work on similar computers that differ in the year of release or version of the operating system,
- applications that are created for a specific type of operating system usually do not work on computers with a different type of operating system,
- different versions of the same application can (and usually do) look and work differently.

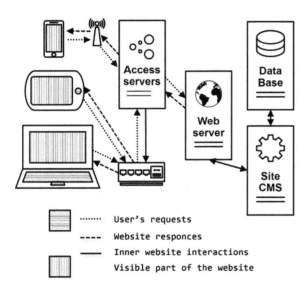

Website Front End

Visible For Visitors

Access servers

Web server

Data Base

Site CMS

……… User's requests
---- Website responces
—— Inner website interactions
Visible part of the website

Do you understand what we are talking about?

The device, its operating system, and the type and version of the browser being used all together form what is conveniently called the client platform, or simply the client.

So, existing clients are different.

The browser through which interaction occurs in the front end is also an application. And for it, everything we have just said is true, too.

Therefore, different browsers can show (and they do show!) a different view of the same web page on devices of different types.

Let's make it shorter and more straightforward.

The client displays the page's content, design, and interactive elements as a result of its interaction with the front end's codes of the site.

26.3. How the front end works

The client can handle the following:
- HTML documents containing structured content,
- document-associated CSS style sheets that define the appearance of the content,
- included in the document or downloadable fragments of Java Script programs that are part of the core of WordPress or come with themes and plugins that provide enhanced interactive features,
- third-party Java Script fragments, such as media players, social network widgets,

or codes for displaying advertising banners.

When you open a web page in a browser, all of the above will be transferred to the browser for processing, display, and user interaction.

Often, to simplify the understanding of the whole picture, it is usually the particular view of site pages called the front-end or even just the entire website.

It depends on the context.

But what about the interface of a CMS like WordPress? Is it front-end or not?

The question is quite reasonable. The interface of the WordPress system itself, which we use to manage the site, is not intended for visitors. It is available only to site staff.

However, technically, the interface of the WordPress system is also front-end.

Its pages differ from the public ones, demand special rights to access them, contain other content, and perform other functions than only content showing.

26.4. How the front end is created

There is a straightforward answer to this question: it is created by that part of the site, which is called the back end.

There are only three ways to create:

- static, in which the finished front-end pages, along with all the content, are stored as HTML documents on the server (host) and transferred to the browser without changes,
- dynamic, in which all the components of future pages are stored as separate fragments in files and the database, and HTML documents are programmatically generated from them, which fully correspond to the user's query parameters,
- combined, in which static elements can be used simultaneously with dynamic ones to form HTML documents.

If you open a site page and save it as a file using the standard browser menu, you can learn many interesting things.

1. Not only will the file be saved in HTML format, which you can open in your browser like a usual page. You will see a directory with the same name next to this file on your hard drive. It will contain numerous files - various images, JavaScript code snippets, CSS stylesheet files, and possibly some other files. These are the front-end components available to you. Look at the contents of this folder and try to understand what all this is intended for.

2. The HTML file you saved and the folder with additional content have specific sizes, usually from tens and hundreds of KByte to several MByte. Look at the volume of the pages of sites you know. Fix these numbers in your memory. This knowledge will be helpful to you as a guide when you optimize the pages of your site.

3. Open the HTML file you saved in your browser in the source view mode. Review the content of the code and try to find recognizable elements in it - the title of the page, its description, the titles of the post and its parts, and links to images. You don't need to learn HTML, CSS, and JS, but you may have to touch them sooner or later. This should not frighten you: nothing is mysterious in them or such that it will be impossible to understand if necessary.

4. Study this page and try to interact with it. Compare the look of this page with how it looks on a real site. You will surely find differences. Some elements may be missing, buttons may not work, forms may not be filled out, and images may not

be displayed. These differences are because the real page is combined as a whole thing, receives part of the content dynamically, and interacts with the server in real-time. All this should provide another part of the site.

As we have already said, this part of the site is called the back end. Without it, the site is practically useless (there is one exception - when the site is entirely static, but this is a subject for a separate discussion, to which we may return later).

There is also a particular type of front-end called a stand-alone front-end. We'll cover it in a Progressive Web Apps discussion.

27

Website back end: what is it

The website's back end is not visible to visitors, but this part is responsible for everything. Therefore, the site owner must understand how the back end works and be able to work with it, keeping the situation under control.

27.1. Back end and WordPress interface

While technically part of the front end, the WordPress interface gives the site owner much control over the back end.

All operations you perform in WordPress result in file changes on the server and database.

Here's what he can do.

1. To add, edit, and delete content of all kinds and types. When you create a post, upload an illustration to the site, or edit or delete it, the WordPress interface interacts with the web server and database server software.

2. To edit service and public information about your site, determine how page addresses are generated, manage the commenting system and how publications are created, and perform many other operations that are not always obvious but always very important.

   A significant part of these operations results in changes to the settings of that part of the back end, which is the WordPress system itself.

3. To add, customize, and remove themes. A theme is the most critical part of a WordPress site. The theme ultimately defines the appearance of the pages of the site and its essential functions.

   We will separately consider the topics in more detail. For now, you need to remember that a theme is, of course, both entries in the database and a separate directory on your server.

   When you install a theme, all of these changes are made on the server. When you configure or delete it, changes are also made.

4. To add, configure and remove plugins. Plugins are almost as important as themes. They are responsible for the site's additional functionality; installing, editing, and deleting them is also work influenced on the back end.

Now, you need to understand that you are acting on the back end through the WordPress interface.

Other aspects of interacting with the back-end using WordPress will be discussed later. On which, in turn, the work of the front end entirely depends.

Actually, this is the process of website management.

27.2. A typical back end structure

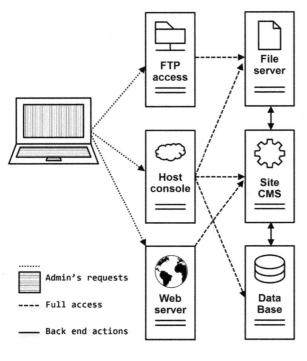

Website Back End Tools

Available For Website Admin

Any hosting provides access to your website's server side, that is, to its back end.

But this access is always limited. We have already discussed this in a chapter dedicated to accessing the server. You will certainly not get access to the system files and directories of the web server software and database because the hoster has no reason to trust his clients and rely on their qualifications.

Of course, if you rent a dedicated hosting server, your access to its resources will be comprehensively complete.

Still, we are talking about virtual or shared hosting - the most massive, affordable, and suitable for most tasks.

When using shared hosting, you will be given access to a very convenient and feature-packed cPanel console. With it, you will manage the back end and solve all the tasks the WordPress interface is not designed to solve.

We will not list them all here but will limit ourselves to a short list of the main features that apply to the site when it is fully configured and working. Here's what you can do:

- use a file manager (to work with backups, upload and download files, create directories and files, access core files, subsystems, WordPress themes, and plugins),
- use a text editor to make changes to the .htaccess system file, WordPress service files (this will be needed already at the WordPress installation stage), and other files,
- create, edit, and delete databases and users,
- get access to the contents of databases to control, resolve problem situations, and create and download backups.

Simply put, you have full access to your WordPress site's file system and database and limited (but fairly complete) access to the host's files and services. Of course, you cannot access the server hardware, but this is for the best.

We will consider a significantly more complete list of cPanel features in a separate chapter.

27.3. Where does the site work - on the front end or on the back end?

Your site runs on both the back end (server) and the front end (client) at the same time.

Modern technologies are such that both parts of your site are connected with each other quite harmoniously and absolutely inextricably. They are inseparable.

Let's try to describe the situation when your site is entirely ready to receive visitors as simply and clearly as possible.

When a visitor finds your site in a search, clicks on a link with the address of a page on your site, or types the site address in the address bar of the browser, his client sends a request (HTTP request) to the server to get the page that matches this address.

The server receives the request, gathers everything related to the page requested by the client (HTML, CSS, JS), calls programs that find the necessary information in the database and generates and sends the resulting document to the client. In fact, different technologies can be used to fulfill the request, but the essence of this does not change.

This concludes the first part of the interaction with the front end.

The client's browser received the page, processed it, and displayed it in its window. If it is provided and possible, the page can independently contact the server to obtain the missing data.

In this case, the page displayed as the front end additionally interacts with the back end without the client's participation.

Two options are possible when a client device user performs actions on a site page.

1. All the data and programs necessary to implement the required actions are already loaded within the page. In this case, interaction with the back end is not needed. All activities are performed directly in the client's browser.

2. The page does not contain all the necessary data and program codes to work with them. In this case, the page accesses the back-end programs, all the required actions are performed on the server, and the page receives the finished result and interprets it following the logic of the work needed.

Various modern technologies perfectly distribute work between the front end and back end. Many WordPress themes and plugins use them. It is essential.

If your site has a lot of visitors, and for the site to work, you need to access the database often, for example, then the load on the server increases. When using shared hosting, this can cause problems with reaching performance limits. As a result, your site will become slower for all visitors, and the host will offer you a more expensive hosting plan.

Suppose the main work of the pages of your site performs the front-end. In that case, you should not unnecessarily overload the pages with visual components, use too complicated layouts, or make pages unnecessarily interactive. This can lead to a loss of browser performance for a particular client, and it's freezing, threatening to lose visitors.

Therefore, it is essential to support a balance between the load on the front-end and back-end. We will consider this separate topic at the stages of creating and operating the site.

Since you now know what we are talking about, we will look at how a WordPress site works in the next chapter.

28

How
a WordPress website
is set up

Like any other site with or without a CMS, a WordPress site is not a box with buttons. A website is, in one way or another, a distributed system.

The back end can be hundreds or thousands of miles from the site owner. Front-end users don't care how far they are from the server.

This should always be remembered: the most important thing, in this case, is that everything starts with the server part.

28.1. What the host looks like before installing WordPress

Once you have purchased hosting services, you can access disk space to host your website. You can get this access using the file manager that is part of the cPanel console.

In a directory called www and directly dedicated to hosting site files, you can find (not always, but in most cases):

- the .well-known directory, which is used by hosting services when connecting an SSL certificate (this directory cannot be renamed or deleted; it is best not to do anything with it),
- the cgi-bin directory, which is traditionally used to store Perl scripts (if you do not plan to use them, you can safely delete the directory, but you can leave it - it is not needed but does not interfere with anything),
- the .htaccess file is the current directory-level configuration file for the web server. You will need it in the future (it can currently be empty or contain several lines automatically added by the server; this file does not need to be edited yet).

Before installing WordPress on a host, you need to:

- connect a domain name,
- install an SSL certificate,
- create a database (after creation, it will be empty),
- create a database user account,
- give the user access to the database.

All this is done using cPanel and does not cause any difficulties. We will do this practically when creating a real site.

In addition to the above, you will have at your disposal disk space and a directory that is specially allocated for placing back-end files.

Then, you need to install WordPress on the host. This can be done using cPanel if hosting capabilities allow it or manually (in my opinion, this is better). We will consider the installation process itself later when creating the site.

Now, we will briefly look at preparing for installation - unpacked WordPress.

28.2. What the host looks like after unpacking WordPress

After unpacking (and further installing), you will see several directories and a fairly large number of files in your directory on the host.

You will not see anything mysterious and surprising; everything is very simple.

The wp-admin directory contains all the core files and data required for the WordPress interface to function. The content of this directory is the most conservative; it is the "core" of WordPress.

The wp-includes directory contains a less conservative part of the files; these are more like add-ons "above the core" of WordPress.

The wp-content directory contains directories and files that are not part of WordPress itself. This directory stores themes, plugins, cached files, activity logs, and much more that can be placed in this directory by the themes and plugins themselves. It also stores data the site administrator uploads using the WordPress interface, such as illustrations.

Except in extraordinary cases, you may not change the contents of these directories or edit the files they contain.

Those extraordinary cases are child theme creation and some emergencies; we'll talk more about that in the future.

In addition, you will see another fifteen files with the .php extension. These are programs that are part of WordPress and are responsible for solving the most important and priority tasks. One of these files, called wp-config-sample.php, you will need to edit and

WP Website Back End Structure

- https://your-site.com/wp-admin/
- Admin
- WP CMS Admin Interface
- Web server
- https://your-site.com/
- Visitor
- Website Public Pages

Server Disk Space

- **Root directory (WWW)**
  - wp-config.php – most important settings
  - other php files – common functionality
- **wp-admin**
  - WP CMS core php files
  - WP CMS interface and auxiliary files
- **wp-includes**
  - WP CMS "above the core" php files
  - Additional libraries, styles, fonts,...
- **wp-content**
  - Themes, plugins, caches, logs
  - All media files uploaded with WP
- **Data Base (MySQL)**
  - Important settings and often changing data
  - All of the site posts and other text data

rename during the installation process. All other files should remain unchanged.

If you look at what happened to the database you created, you will find that tables have appeared in it, and records have appeared in the tables. The WordPress installer has fully prepared the database for work.

We do not describe or study the process of installing WordPress itself. This will be done later, at the stage of the actual creation of the site. We are now in the introductory phase.

28.3. Where is WordPress really?

Everything is simple.

If your site opens at https://your-site.com, the WordPress interface should be accessed at https://your-site.com/wp-admin/.

After installation and entering your username and password, you will see the WordPress interface on the screen. At first glance, it is pretty diverse and slightly unclear, but this is only the first impression.

So, after installing WordPress, you will have four addresses that you will need to work with the site:

- *https://your-site.com* - the main page of your site; it will be visible to the whole world (if you see fit, you can hide all pages of your site for the period of its preparation for launch using a special plugin),
- *https://your-site.com/wp-admin/* - the address of the main page of the WordPress CMS interface, which is available to you using the login and password that you chose during the WordPress installation,
- the address of access to the client account on your host, with which you can manage hosting services and communicate with the support service,
- the address of access to the cPanel console (often the cPanel console is available via a link in the client account interface on the hosting, but this is not always the case) with your username and password, with which you can manage the back-end of the site.

You will learn how to manage a WordPress site in the next chapter.

29

How to manage
a WordPress site

Running a WordPress site means doing quite a lot of things. It is necessary to perform tasks that may seem unrelated to each other. But this is only at first glance.

We will briefly describe the main of these works so that you can better navigate what is happening on the site and around it in the future.

29.1. How to manage a website using CMS WordPress

You will have to deal with the WordPress interface for more than just preparing and publishing posts.

There are stages such as the initial setup stage, the advanced setup stage, the theme and plugin installation stage, and the operational stage. Each stage can be characterized by particular tasks and ways to solve them.

29.1.1. Website setup right after installing WordPress

This is the easiest and most apparent setup step.

At this stage, works are usually performed, which are implied: specifying the name of the site and its brief description (tagline), setting up administrator data, and creating additional accounts (if necessary).

In addition, language settings, time zone selected, date, and time formats are checked and, if necessary, corrected. All these settings can be edited at any time, and they primarily relate to the organization of work with the site.

29.1.2. Advanced WordPress settings

These settings are important not only for organizing work with the site. They can influence its future perception by the outside world, including search engines.

When configuring post settings, you must consider the type of editor to be used or preferred (block or classic; we will consider this important issue in a separate chapter), the post format, and whether it belongs to the "default" site category.

Proper setup will save you time and avoid wrong actions.

The Reading options are critical; among them is the checkbox to prevent search engines from indexing the site.

If your site is not ready and does not contain quality content, this checkbox must be activated (unless you requested this option during the WordPress installation).

Pay special attention to the Permalinks settings. These settings need to be done once and never changed again.

Changing their format when search engines already index your site will lead to a deterioration in its position. We will also consider this issue separately.

29.1.3. Installing themes and plugins

If your site is not yet ready for publication and you have disabled its indexing, you need to make it inaccessible to visitors urgently.

Of course, they don't need to see a half-finished product. This is easy to do using a specialized plugin; in due time, we will see how to select and configure it in due time.

The second important aspect of your job is security. On the WordPress side, there are also a variety of solutions in the form of plugins for this.

The third problem to deal with at the outset is installing and configuring a theme that suits your needs.

The fourth important issue is ensuring SEO. It is a very versatile problem, consisting of many tasks. And for it, there are plugins with which we will get acquainted.

Installing plugins and themes is quite simple; we will cover this in separate chapters at the site creation stage.

After all these questions are answered, you will be ready to start filling your site with content.

29.2. Operational stage

Every new site owner is impatient.

He wants to disable the plugin as soon as possible, which shows only the inscription "Under Construction" instead of brilliant content and colorful pages.

That is because the site owner expects special treatment from the entire world (including search engines). And an immediate success, of course.

Do not hurry. The world is gigantic, and users are overly spoiled by information abundance.

Prepare your site carefully for launch. Start its operation in a "closed" mode and meticulously study the content, functions, and design.

Then, improve your site.

No one can achieve complete perfection, so for the end of the polishing stage, your best adviser is a calendar.

Finish preparing the site by the deadline.

If you don't have enough time, move the deadline by the days you need, but don't try to do everything "tomorrow."

At this stage, you will do the next:
- add and remove plugins, experiment with them, and check their work,
- change and customize themes, redo the placement of information blocks,
- customize page design options,
- test the site on different devices,
- repeat all of the above in various combinations until the day the site is opened for users.

Start this stage by creating a complete backup of your database and all site files and downloading it all to your computer. It will be better this way.

Once your site is open to visitors, your work will become more routine (but not dull, you will see).

Experimenting with settings, design, and changing themes and plugins at this stage is risky, and some experiments can harm the site.

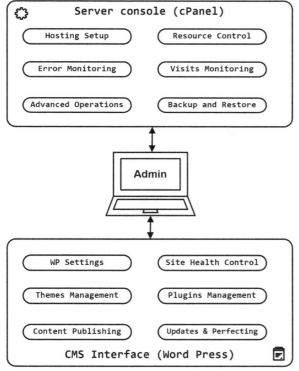

At this stage, you will have other worries:

- regularly adding new and updating old content,
- sending updates for indexing to search engines,
- periodic backup of the database and all site files,
- installation of WordPress updates (it is updated regularly, and before each update, it is better to have a full backup of the site),
- installing plugin updates,
- install theme updates,
- installation of translation updates (if you use other languages),
- site health monitoring and troubleshooting,
- monitoring errors when accessing the site and eliminating their causes,
- monitoring hacking attempts or unauthorized access to the site and taking action.

It's not as difficult as it might seem. In addition, not only WordPress is at your disposal, but also cPanel and even a hosting support service.

29.3. How to manage your website with hosting tools

29.3.1. Website hosting initial setup

Just like with WordPress, the initial server-side setup will deal with access and security issues.

There isn't much work to do here. Hosting is a fairly versatile and well-established service (unlike your new site). Many server-side issues have already been resolved by a system administrator whose name you will likely never know.

If you choose a hosting that suits your needs, you will not have any problems.

Here is what you will have to do on the server side (complete, but short, list of tasks):
- connect a domain name and wait for its delegation,
- get (or buy) and install an SSL certificate and wait for the domain to be available via a secure protocol,
- make the necessary changes to the .htaccess file.
- install WordPress,
- configure (if applicable) hosting components responsible for protection and security.

29.3.2. Work with the site host during the operation phase

If everything is done correctly, then at the site operation stage, you will have only four tasks that will need to be solved on the host side using the tools available to you in the cPanel console.

29.3.2.1. Monitoring the resources used by the site

If your site often and regularly exceeds the limits of the resources allocated to it - RAM, processor power, the number of requests, the amount of data transferred - then the hoster will advise you to upgrade the tariff plan, or even can turn off your site so that you became more compliant.

Yes, it happens. But only if the site is poorly optimized, CDN and server cache are not used, the flow of visitors has skyrocketed, and you did not take care in advance that this would not cause a peak load on the server.

We will study this issue in detail - and you will not have such trouble.

29.3.2.2. Monitoring site access errors

The visitor may get upset and leave if errors occur when accessing the site. Well, if he comes back to your site, say, tomorrow. But he may never return at all, which is terrible.

But if this is not just a visitor but a search bot, then your site will begin to gain penalty points in the search engine database, and this is fraught with a loss of positions in the search and, as a result, traffic. This isn't good too.

Therefore, error monitoring should be performed regularly. First - daily, then - as needed.

Each error is the subject of analysis and the reason for finding a solution to the problem.

The site should work without errors.

29.3.2.3. Monitoring data about visitors and visits

This information can and should be checked even more frequently than the error log.

Site visitors are not only search engine bots and decent people who are sincerely interested in the subject of your publications.

Among the visitors, there is a surprisingly large variety of burglars, scammers, and other intruders. They will try to steal your login password, find vulnerabilities in plugins and themes, inject their code into the database, or do something else in the same vein.

Sometimes, the activities of such characters are surprising - it seems that many of them themselves do not know why they need to do all this.

But it does not change anything. The site needs to be protected.

Since attack methods are well known, one of the ways to detect attacks early is to analyze the statistics of site visits on the server.

This is not difficult. We will consider this issue in more detail when working with a ready-made site. Just record this critical moment in your memory and workbook for now.

29.3.3. Working with backups

There are many ways to work with backups.

Some will say there are even special WordPress plugins for this, and you shouldn't bother working on the server side.

Someone will say that regular backups with the ability to restore the site are entirely a service included in the paid hosting package.

But what if a plugin is rendered useless because the WordPress interface is no longer available due to plugin incompatibility with the theme, a problem with the caching system, or a failed update?

But what if you have made many changes to the site and published new content since the scheduled backup, which the host automatically created, and you don't want to lose it all?

You probably already guessed how to answer these questions correctly.

You need to be able and able to create a full backup of the site when you need it, and not just when it is scheduled.

You need to have the latest backup in case of any failure or accident and be able to restore your site from it completely.

You need complete control over the situation and absolute confidence that your site is invulnerable because the backup was created by you personally, and you know exactly when and how it was done, and you can recreate your site from it.

All this sounds very serious and even frightening, but the reality is actually more straightforward.

When I teach you how to make backup copies and recreate a site from them, you will see that this can be done in a matter of minutes with the help of simple manipulations.

We will cover these works in detail in the future.

This will give you confidence and protect you from problems.

30

What is
a WordPress Theme

What is a WordPress Theme? This question is usually answered that this is a set of files that define the website's appearance. This is an incomplete answer.

Surprisingly, the WordPress developer himself does not give an exact and complete answer to this question. At least there is no such answer here: ***https://developer.wordpress.org/themes/getting-started/what-is-a-theme/****.*

We will get the most complete and accurate answer to this question. It will reflect my personal point of view, which I consider, of course, absolutely correct.

Keep in mind that the developers of the WordPress CMS itself offer very few of their own-made themes, which are traditionally named after the release year.

All the other many thousands of themes (and plugins) are created by third-party developers. This is part of the incredibly successful WordPress business model.

30.1. Definition of a WordPress theme

First, let's agree on terminology. A set of files is too general a concept, and it is not ordered in any way. A rather convenient term is a component as a part of a larger composite whole.

So, a theme is a component. According to the information on the developer's site, changing this component leads to a change in the appearance of the site, or rather, the front end, which is available to the visitor.

In addition, the theme should not contain, according to the WordPress developers, "critical functionality." It is difficult to argue with this, but precise definitions are still more practical. Here, for now, we note that the functionality of a theme is limited by the capabilities of its elements.

It's not explicitly stated anywhere, but keep in mind that a theme is a required component, unlike a plugin. That is, your site may not have a single plugin, but the theme must be installed.

No theme - no front end, no site itself.

Definition: A theme is a mandatory component of a site built on the WordPress CMS, designed for front-end visualization, providing visual structuring, logical ordering, and design of the appearance of information elements and blocks included in it, as well as processing site user interactions with these elements and blocks.

With my love for complete definitions, it turned out a little cumbersome.

All other details are, in one way or another, additional characteristics of the theme's properties, which reflect the specialization of the theme, its focus on various client devices, compatibility with other components, and customization options.

30.2. WordPress theme properties

Each theme includes at least one layout for each page type: for the home/blog page, category page, post page, and standalone page.

Page layouts can have a variety of visual layouts, from a simple one-column layout for a landing page to a multi-column layout for a large information site homepage.

Page layouts can be adapted to varying degrees for display on different types of devices with different screen widths.

Page layouts can, in various combinations, include:
- the main information field (for the feed of publications, post or page content, and search results) is required, and it can have multiple columns,
- page title field (there may be more than one),
- page footer field (can be more than one, in one or more columns),
- additional columns.

Generally speaking, the variety of page layout options is such that it makes no sense to list them all.

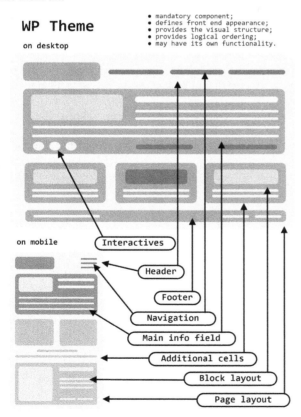

Look at the logo of this site, placed on the illustrations in the posts: it shows one of the options for the classic layout of the site page.

Page layout cells contain information units and blocks of information units. The division into units and blocks is very conditional. To begin with, let's assume, for example, that a short representation of a post on the site's main page is an information unit, and the entire feed of publications is a block of information units.

An even smaller component is the element of the information unit (title, illustration, description text).

All of the above have colors, the text has typefaces, and individual inscriptions may differ in size and alignment. Padding, margins, background color, menu bar color, link highlighting, etc.

You need to be able to manage all this.

Most themes provide such opportunities, but they are not always enough. We will learn how to get out of this situation when we customize the appearance of the newly created site.

Now we can say what the requirement of the WordPress development team that does not allow the theme developer to contribute "critical functionality" to it really means.

30.3. WordPress theme features

We have listed all the components of the layouts that any WordPress theme is responsible for.

These components limit the range of functions and capabilities that a theme can have. Everything that goes beyond the scope of the theme should not be the object of interference from its settings and functions. Otherwise, theme developers can very quickly turn WordPress into a broken system with their tweaks and interventions.

So, it is customary that the main place where you can get acquainted with the theme and download it for installation (or install it directly from the WordPress interface) is the official site ***https://wordpress.org***. Everything uploaded there for distribution to system users is carefully checked in many ways.

This is perhaps the only totally reliable source for themes and plugins to download and install on the site.

If you installed your theme from an official source, then it will not violate the developer's requirements.

As for the possibilities of individual topics, they can be very different. The production of themes is a separate developed industry that has accumulated a variety of products.

For all the types of sites we reviewed in the preceding chapters, there are a lot of ready-to-use themes equipped with everything you need. Our task is just to choose a theme whose layouts and features suit us best.

What's especially important for beginners is that a lot of great themes are available free of charge.

You can read more about themes here: ***https://wordpress.org/support/article/using-themes/***.

All tasks, functions, and features that are not available to themes are solved with the help of plugins.

31

What is
a WordPress plugin

What is a WordPress Plugin? This question most often, as in the case of themes, you can get a correct but incomplete answer. It is commonly said that a plugin is a package of codes that extends the functionality of a WordPress site.

In principle, this is true, but not the whole truth.

As in the case of themes, we will give an absolutely exact and complete definition. But first, let's look at what we know about plugins.

31.1. How to install a WordPress plugin

The plugin is installed in the same way as the theme.

To install, you can use the built-in installer, which allows you to find the plugin you need on the official WordPress website and immediately install and activate it.

For installation, you can use third-party sources, install plugins manually on the server side, and install plugins from zipped files through the WordPress interface.

We recommend the first method in all cases. It guarantees the installed plugin's security and compliance with the system developers' requirements.

The last method, installation through the WordPress interface from the zipped file - is recommended when you have purchased a premium version of a plugin you know, obtained from the official WordPress site.

Premium plugins are distributed by their creators in this way.

Their sale is not provided on the official WordPress website since the system developers do not participate in sales.

Like with themes, WordPress developers have developed and maintained a small number of plugins.

But their plugins are secure and feature-rich (except the "Hello Dolly" plugin, which is completely useless and has become a traditional part of the WordPress culture).

Once installed, the plugin, just like the theme, becomes part of the back end of your website. Just like a theme, it can contain different types of files.

Unlike a theme, a plugin is not a functionally required component.

If the capabilities of the kernel and the installed theme are enough for you, security issues are totally resolved on the host side, and the speed of the site suits you, then you can quite do without plugins at all.

But that doesn't happen.

There wouldn't be so many plugins if they weren't needed. It's all about the diversity of their features that suit the needs of site owners.

31.2. Features and purposes of WordPress plugins

As already mentioned, plugins are designed to enhance the capabilities of WordPress by adding features that are not contained in the core system.

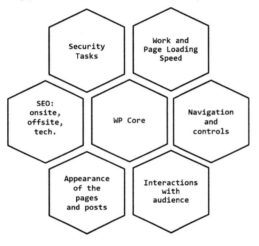

The nature of the added features, in essence, is not limited by anything except the imagination of the plugin developer and the composition of the tasks to be solved.

Since both have an infinite number of options, there are a lot of plugins, tens of thousands of them only in the official repository at ***https://wordpress.org/plugins/***.

Plugins can:

*   add information units and blocks to page layouts,
*   optimize the pages and files of the site,
*   create new taxonomies and fully organize work with them,
*   manage access to the materials and components of the site.

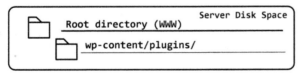

It is a general shortlist showing that plugins can do almost anything.

To make it easier for you to navigate the plugins, here is a rough list of their specializations:

*   optimization of files and pages of the site (reduction in size and exclusion of unnecessary),
*   optimization of loading processes of site pages and third-party content,
*   page caching (creating ready-made static images of site pages),
*   protection against unauthorized access, spam in comments, hacking, and other attacks,
*   providing solutions to SEO problems.
*   integration with search engines,
*   integration with attendance analysis systems,

- integration with advertising display systems,
- integration with social networks,
- expanding interactivity and improving site navigation,
- adding feedback forms and tools for communication with visitors,
- providing a solution to the problem of e-mail marketing,
- creating marketplaces for conventional and digital goods and affiliated,
- organizing acceptance of payments and processing of purchases,
- embedding third-party content (videos, widgets, feeds),
- multilingual support,
- management of internal codes of pages and additional types of internal markup.

Over time, you will be able to expand this list by yourself.

31.3. WordPress plugin definition

We agreed on terminology in a previous chapter on themes. The capabilities and purpose of the plugins have just been described above.

We are ready to define a plugin.

Definition: A plugin is an optional component of a site built on the WordPress CMS, designed to add features related to improving the quality of the site's functioning as a technical system, achieving the site's goals, and interacting with external resources and with the site's audience.

It turned out a little shorter than the definition of the theme - due to a broader range of possibilities.

A plugin, of course, cannot replace a theme. However, there are also exceptional cases.

Some themes contain almost no features, have virtually no custom design features, and therefore cannot be fully used "out-of-the-box."

Such themes began to appear after adding the "block editing" feature to WordPress.

The block content editor Gutenberg has been part of the WordPress system since version 5.0.

We will touch on this topic in more detail in the next post - about patterns.

For now, commit to memory that these "blank" themes are created by the developers of "page builders" for WordPress, which are, you guessed it, plugins.

With the help of such plugins and "blank" themes, you can create websites that look original and can be adapted to the requirements of a customer who wants to achieve an exact match between the look of the site and the requirements of his brand book.

We will consider this issue in more detail when creating the site.

31.4. How many plugins can a WordPress site have?

This question is quite popular with beginners.

The correct answer is as follows: as much as necessary to solve specific problems and nothing more.

As practice shows, for a small information site, you need the following:

- protection, firewall, virus scanner, log analyzer - 1 ... 3 plugins,
- page loading optimization and caching - 2...4,
- SEO - 1...2 (free version or free and paid versions of one plugin),
- additional navigation and interactivity on the site - 2...3,
- integration with social networks - 1..2,
- integration with search engines - 1...2,

- work with popup forms - 1…2,
- work with email - 1 … 2,
- content editing - 1 plugin (classic editor),
- work with hyperlinks - 1…2,
- plugins for notifying of the website cookies and privacy policy - 1…2 plugins.

So, a small site could have 13 to 22 plugins based on this list. In reality, there may be more of them, but usually, there are excessive ones among them.

These are not recommendations but rather just statistics I'd collected while working with my own and other people's sites.

In any case, redundant and unused plugins should be removed without hesitation. If you are not using any plugin, make it inactive. If the need for it does not return after that for some time - just remove it.

Some plugins, even excellent ones, can slow down your site.

Beginners love to install dozens of plugins and experiment with them. Don't ever do that. It is pretty easy to find a plugin, even on the official WordPress website, which can leave unnecessary information garbage in the system after its removal.

Unused, inactive plugins (like themes, too) are potential vulnerabilities on your site.

32

What is
a WordPress pattern

The WordPress pattern is a relatively new component type introduced with the December 2018 release of WordPress 5.0. This is due to the introduction of block content editing technology.

It was in this version of WordPress that the Gutenberg block editor appeared.

This technology is intended for people with little experience who prefer the visual construction of content.

In addition, this way of editing allows for more flexibility and accuracy in matching page design to the requirements of a particular brand.

It is very convenient to use block editing technology if there is a need for original and non-standard visual blocks. Such blocks are very diverse and decorative; they can be placed in different places on page layouts.

32.1. WordPress pattern definition

Patterns can be used for different purposes.

Hundreds of patterns are available for download on the official WordPress website at *https://wordpress.org/patterns/*.

A pattern is an entirely independent component. It is inserted into the page by simple copy and paste through the clipboard and has no links to WordPress core.

In addition, many of the blocks available in the Gutenberg block editor are patterns or very close to them.

Definition: A pattern is an optional component of a website built with the WordPress CMS, a ready-to-use information block with a pre-configured design, designed for arbitrary placement in page layouts, retaining its appearance regardless of the theme used and allowing customization and editing using the content block editor.

The various page builders come with their own set of patterns.

Therefore, if you need visual diversity and the original design of the site pages, this is an excellent solution for you.

If you have a large amount of content of the same type in structure, and the site is more informational than image and not advertising, then in that case, patterns may come in handy in a small number of situations or even may not be necessary at all.

Interestingly, since version 5.0, which included the Gutenberg block editor for the first time, the WordPress developer has excluded the classic version of the content editor, also known as TinyMCE, from the distribution.

32.2. Gutenberg block editor vs classic TinyMCE editor

Gutenberg Editor is, actually, a middle ground between a regular editor and visual page builders (which are available as plugins).

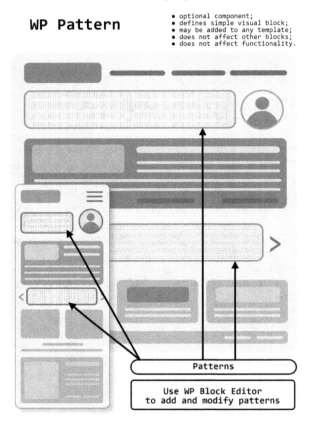

WP Pattern

- optional component;
- defines simple visual block;
- may be added to any template;
- does not affect other blocks;
- does not affect functionality.

Patterns

Use WP Block Editor
to add and modify patterns

This editor allows, by manipulating blocks, to construct genuinely diverse and visually rich pages, but it is inferior in terms of pre-rendering capabilities to specialized page builders.

On the other hand, it provides almost all the features of a classic editor but is notably less convenient for everyday work on a blog, magazine, or collection of thematic reviews, where the main content is text.

Therefore, among the plugins published on the WordPress site, the plugin Classic Editor (also developed by the WordPress team) is the undisputed leader in downloads and is installed by the owners of all sites that work with text content.

You will likely have such a need. This is normal; both editors coexist perfectly, and we will return to this issue at the site creation stage.

After installing the classic editor plugin, you need to make a few simple settings on the system so that using both editors (or just the classic one) is convenient for you.

32.3. Who else is interested in pattern technology

Of course, this technology is of interest to developers.

I mean website developers in the first place.

If your goal is to learn how to create and maintain WordPress sites for customers, then pattern technology is one of the key points for you. Clients love a personalized approach to page design, and with the help of patterns and work in the Gutenberg Editor (or using the page builder plugin and its block library), you can please the most capricious client.

In doing so, you will stay within the WordPress technology and be able to work very quickly and efficiently.

Pattern technology is perhaps the most accessible to beginner WordPress component developers. Patterning is much easier than a self-developed plugin or a "real" (not child) theme and can be the first step in your developer journey. You can find the required documentation here: ***https://developer.wordpress.org/block-editor/reference-guides/block-api/block-patterns/***.

Anyway, it's worth a try.

If you are not ready for this and intend to continue the path to creating your first site with your own hands, then we will continue this topic in posts dedicated to classic and block editors.

33

What is
the Classic WordPress editor

The classic WordPress editor, also known as TinyMCE (Moxiecode Content Editor), was released in 2004 and was included in version 2.0 of WordPress in 2005.

Since then, it has been known as the "Classic WordPress Editor."

As of version 5.0, released in December 2018, it has been replaced with the Gutenberg block editor. Then, the "classic editor" returned as a plugin.

33.1. Why should we discuss the classic WordPress editor

Why are we talking about this, and why should we consider these editors at all?

There are severe reasons to consider both these editors and not in comparison. These reasons are due to the purpose and features of these somewhat different products.

In addition, there is another important reason: the content editor is the part of the CMS that you will use much more often than all the other parts of it.

Therefore, it is beneficial to have at least a general idea of the editor before actually working with it.

That's why we're discussing the classic editor.

1. The classic editor is ideal for working with site content, especially if the site is informational. This tool is for everyday use; therefore, you must know its functions and features well.
2. The classic text editor does not exist on its own. Apart from the editor window, there are many things on the content editing page. It is necessary to understand why all this is needed and how to work with it.
3. The classic text editor is very similar to all the editors you have dealt with before. But it has some non-obvious features that are very important. Something you might think of as just text formatting can make all the difference to the fate of your site.

33.2. What are around the text edit box

On the left side of the window, you have access to the standard WordPress menu, which allows you to navigate through all the functions and components of the system.

In the upper part of the window, there is a curtain with settings for displaying interface elements.

Among these elements, some may be absolutely necessary for you. For example, blocks with SEO information, the Structured Data Types edit box, the Excerpts edit box, and much more.

WP Classic Editor

Carefully review the complete list of blocks and fields and customize their display according to your needs.

At the bottom of the window is everything you just set up with the top curtain.

In the right part of the window are mandatory publication settings blocks: availability, date and time of creation and publication, linking to categories, linking to tags, choosing the main illustration, and more.

Please note: It is in the right part of the window that there are possible changes and additions related to the features of the theme used and a number of essential plugins.

33.3. Content editing tools and modes

It is much more accurate to call the classic WordPress editor a content editor, of course.

This is true for any modern "text editor" because such editors have long allowed you to insert into text and edit a wide variety of objects that are not text - drawings, diagrams, photographs, and much more.

Our "classic editor" is no exception.

In terms of its capabilities, it is far superior to a regular text editor but inferior to advanced code editors. But he can work in two modes.

The "Visual" mode is reminiscent of the familiar WYSIWYG editing method when all the subtleties of formatting immediately become visible.

This is very important, for example, when structuring your post with headings. In this mode, you have access to a toolbar with formatting tools that look pretty familiar.

Yes, this is very convenient, but there are two points that you just need to keep in mind.

1. If you paste pre-formatted text through the clipboard in this mode (for example, from MS Word or the Google Drive text editor), formatting codes will also be copied and pasted along with the text.

   This can lead to unpleasant and unpredictable results - formatting codes from third-party editors simply may not match what is provided by the theme you are using on the site.

   Such codes will become informational garbage that you will have to remove manually.

2. What you see in this mode adequately reflects the structure of the content but does not match how the content will look on the site.

To do this, you need to use the "View Post" link or open the post's page on the site if the post has already been published or the "Preview" link if the post has not yet been published.

As you already understand, it is convenient to work in this mode, but you need to be able to make detailed checks and edits. There is another editing mode for this.

This is the "Text" mode, which is indispensable when you need to keep the situation under complete control.

In this mode, you can safely paste your texts with or without pre-formatting - they will be copied without unnecessary codes. You can switch to "Visual" mode and format the text how you want.

In this mode, you can see and, if necessary, edit all formatting codes, remove random errors, and add your codes.

Little secret: You can even paste the WordPress Pattern Codes we talked about a while ago.

Why is everything so complicated, you ask?

Everything is not so complicated, and there are no artificial complications here. Pretty soon, you will learn to understand the difference between these modes and will easily switch between them as needed.

This is the main thing you need to understand now. Finally, two little tricks.

33.4. Two practical tips for working in the classic editor

1. If you want to create a bulleted or numbered list in "Visual" mode, you must first create its body - separate list lines.

If you are a fan of office word processors, then out of habit, you can use the "soft" newline (Shift + Enter) to form the body of the list.

Then, you select the list body with the mouse and press the list formatting button on the toolbar, and... nothing happens.

More precisely, you will get a list of one item, which will include all your lines.

Use only a regular line feed (Enter) to break text, not a "soft" one!

2. If you want to insert some third-party codes in "Text" mode, and they turn out to contain non-standard or special characters (which happens in straightforward cases, for example, when it comes to curly brackets, angle brackets, and some apostrophes - which should be displayed on the site as text), you do not need to switch to "Visual" mode before saving or publishing a post.

In some cases, simply switching to "Visual" mode will corrupt such codes.

Therefore, to avoid wasting time and attention on a list of secondary technical information now, just remember this.

When you need to insert codes into a post, you can control the fate of such codes by simply switching between editing modes.

If the codes break when switching to "Visual" mode, then save and publish your post in "Text" mode.

The classic editor is a very powerful tool.

We will consider its capabilities in more detail at the stage of creating a site.

34

What is
the WordPress Block Editor

The Gutenberg block editor, which became part of the WordPress core in December 2018, is a fantastic tool in its capabilities.
It makes visual diversity possible while maintaining the style and design canons, even for pages and publications that are simple in content and design.

34.1. What is the difference between the Gutenberg editor and the classic editor

As I promised you, we will not be comparing these editors.

Of course, he also knows how to perform text editing functions and link a post to a category and tags, but the similarity ends there. This editor does a lot more and does everything totally differently.

Just accept it as it is: the Gutenberg block editor is a totally different editor. Completely different!

From the features of this editor, its difference in purpose follows: it is less adapted than the classic editor to solve problems of producing a large number of publications of the same type in structure.

But it allows you to create posts with a complex design, elements, and blocks inside that are diverse in nature and purpose.

This editor is more of a tool for designing publications than for mass production.

If your site does not have a lot of publications that are diverse in structure and functions, then this editor will suit you perfectly.

34.2. How the Gutenberg editor works

The fundamental novelty lies in the fact that when creating a post, you must first select the type of block and insert it in the desired place in the publication, and then fill the block with content and, if necessary, refine its settings.

As you remember, in the classic editor, you first had to create content, and only after that deal with its formatting and design.

In the case of the block editor, as you can see, the opposite is true.

To insert into a post, you can use any of the blocks from the standard core set of

WP Block Editor

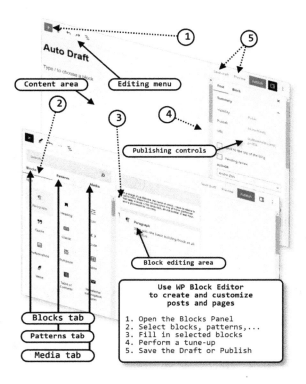

WordPress.

These blocks are: paragraph, title, subtitle, quote, image, gallery, video, audio, columns, file, code, list, and button.

It is important to note that this editor allows you to use images in very diverse ways, including as backgrounds with a parallax effect.

Of course, there is nothing fundamentally new in this list. Fundamentally new is the possibility of visual and easy work, which even a novice site administrator can handle.

In principle, this editor is suitable for replacing the classic one in the "Code Editor" mode. Yes, this editor, like the classic one, has two modes of operation: "Visual Editor" and "Code Editor."

Of course, choosing between a classic editor and a block editor is a matter of habit and personal taste.

From my point of view, the block editor would greatly benefit if it had another mode - the same as the visual editing mode in the classic editor. This would make the block editor much more capable of handling a large number of predominantly text publications.

34.3. Additional blocks for the Gutenberg editor

With all the variety of blocks of this editor, users, of course, have needs that go beyond this diversity.

Nothing is surprising. This is exactly the case when growing needs under the influence of the market meet with the possibilities of their immediate satisfaction.

These features are easily achievable in the form of downloadable plugins with additional blocks for the Gutenberg editor (as you should look for them among the plugins on the official WordPress site).

Some themes and plugins may also add custom blocks to the collection available on your site.

For example, an SEO plugin can add block options for visualizing Structured Data Types (recipes, reviews, how-to, and more), a social plugin - blocks with social network buttons, and a podcast plugin - widgets for playing sound recordings).

In general, this editor dramatically expands the possibilities for creativity. The main thing is not to get too carried away with the variety of blocks so as not to worsen the page load time.

34.4. How to use the Gutenberg editor with the classic editor

It's elementary. Select *Settings | Writing*, set the default editor, and choose whether you want the ability to switch between editors.

If you have specified the ability to switch, the corresponding items will appear in the quick action blocks in the list of posts on the site and the interfaces of both editors.

35

How to publish content and what to do next

How and when should you publish your content?

There are different possible answers to this question. They all relate to your capabilities, intentions, plans, and goals. All of them are related to the destiny you want for your site.

Mechanically, the publishing process is completely understandable: the text is written, illustrations are selected and prepared, and the post is created, designed, and formatted.

It remains only to click the "Publish" button, right?

No, not like this. More precisely, not quite so.

35.1. You need a content plan

Let's assume that your site is fully configured and ready to go.

It functions perfectly, its pages open quickly, and there are no problems that content experts, SEO specialists, marketers, and SMM managers could point out to you. Do you know why they don't see any problems?

Because they haven't seen your content plan. You may have never seen it before. too, which is a good enough reason to immediately begin addressing this issue when you finish reading this post.

Your content plan is a reflection of your site's business model in a content mirror (well said). It cannot be that you do not think about what, in what time frame, in what volume, and with what frequency you will publish on your site.

But a business plan, even if you have it and it was developed in strict accordance with the recommendations of world leaders in business consulting, is only your intention.

Your business plan is unknown and indifferent to search engines and social networks, bookmarking services, directories, forums, video hosting, instant messengers, and all other sources of traffic and backlinks.

This plan cannot affect the promotion of your site in any way, its position in the rankings, the position number in the search engine results, and the average number of unique visitors per day.

As a result, it cannot affect the actual monetization of your site.

All this can be affected (and really is affected!) only by the practical implementation of

Content Plan

Why do you need a content plan?

Plan ▷ Content ▷ Traffic ▷ Profit

Content Plan Types

① Thematic sites and blogs; bloggers and small teams	② Sites with a lot of content; professional teams	③ Sites that support sales; professional teams
Infinite	**Modular**	**Limited**

Content Plan Data Sources

Keyword Search Stats		Seasonal Fluctuations and Trends
	Website Semantic Core	
Target Audience Interests		Competitor posts on websites and social media

the content plan.

Even if you only publish properly prepared content on your site and do nothing else, the site traffic will grow.

The rules are very simple.

1. No traffic - no income.
2. No content - no traffic.
3. No content plan - no content.

You will say that this is not a problem; the Internet is full of materials on how to prepare a content plan and dozens and hundreds of ideas for incredibly attractive posts on various topics. And indeed, it is.

The main thing is that you understand - these materials and ideas result from someone's work implementing a business plan. The people who created this content fulfilled their content plan, and their posts got your attention.

If you do not have a plan you have compiled yourself, without looking at other people's patterns and who knows whose ideas, you are in the wrong way. But it is not bad enough to give up. Sketch a content plan and bring it to a working state; you will still have time to adjust it to a formal standard.

Since you have decided to create a website, you already know what its publications will be about. This is half the battle. You have risen on the wings of your imagination and invented everything.

And... you hung somewhere up there, like a motor piston in a "dead center."

This means you just need a little push to keep moving in the right direction.

Here it is.

35.2. Determine the scope and growth rate of your project

The main unit for measuring the size of your site is not Mbyte.

And not the total duration of the video on its pages, even if you are a videographer. And not the total number of galleries and images in them, even if you are a photographer or an artist. And not the total number of recipes if you are a food blogger.

The main unit for measuring the size of your site is the URL, i.e., the post page address. One post is one URL. How many posts are on the site - so many lines in the sitemap, which is processed by the search robot.

Web crawlers love large, regularly updated sitemaps that lead them to new posts with unique content.

How many posts should be on the site, and how often should new ones be added and old ones updated?

Of course, there are no universal recipes. However, some guidelines will help you understand what kind of content plan you need and how many lines it will contain for posts and columns to update and promote them.

35.2.1. Websites with an infinite content plan

I know successful websites that only 1-2 individuals have worked on for several years.

There will probably always be such sites. Their themes are diverse - cooking, lifestyle, travel, fashion, DIY, and much more. The typical volume of such sites is up to several thousand posts, and the typical regular income from banner advertising is from several thousand to several tens of thousands of dollars per month.

The content plan of such sites usually exists at the very initial stage of work. It quickly becomes clear that the main limitation is life itself, which is written about on such sites by their authors.

New posts on such sites are first published daily (and even more than one per day), then several times a week, weekly, and then become fairly rare.

This is not due to the laziness of the site owners. It's just that every topic, every link profile, and every set of social media profiles eventually has its reach limit. Beyond this limit, audience and traffic growth first slow down, then cease unrelated to the number of posts published.

Therefore, the owners of such sites often shift their activity, for example, to produce videos for driving traffic from new sources.

Such sites can exist and successfully monetize for a long time if several reliable traffic sources exist.

35.2.2. Sites with a modular content plan

Usually, these are publisher websites, sometimes associated with magazines or other printed publications.

Since such sites have a fairly large staff, their content creation follows thematic categories. A topic is selected for which many posts are created.

They get traffic just like any regular website.

When traffic on a given topic stops growing, the staff switches to another topic.

This may go on for many years.

Such sites can have tens and hundreds of thousands of posts, the list of which increases daily by several units or several tens of units.

With so many lines in the sitemap, total traffic from search engines is almost guaranteed to be quite high.

35.2.3. Sites with a limited content plan

The content plan of such sites is initially limited and involves an increase in the number of posts only for the subsequent filling of some thematic gaps or in connection with some events on the site's subject.

This approach is typical for sites related to the release of books, training courses, developing new applications, and solving specific business problems.

This site just has a limited content plan (if we talk about the three main categories) because it has a training course and a book associated with it. There are no endless courses and endless books.

Although, of course, the owners of such sites strive to have categories in which new posts could be constantly published.

This is necessary to obtain and retain search traffic, right?

35.2.4. Choose a content plan type or invent your own

You already understand everything, aren't you?

The implementation of the content plan is limited only to your capabilities. The Internet will eat and digest any amount of content. Just estimate your power.

35.3. Avoid the "survivor bias"

When you are planning to get started, you explore other sites. This is fine. This is a separate work, and we will return to it later when you are already at the stage of owning the created website and when you can treat the matter more professionally.

Now, you are just starting your journey. You already know the theme of your site, have chosen domain name options for it, have a description of its structure, and a draft semantic core, and you feel ready to go.

Look carefully at the sites that attracted you in some way. Check their social media profiles. Pay attention to the dates of the most recent publications and determine whether work is ongoing on these sites or not.

Your task is to understand which sites you like are still active and which ones have already turned into ghosts in which the Internet is so rich. Don't confuse them with survivors!

Examine the existing sites, and imagine that these are your competitors. You will have to get used to the role of their competitor. Otherwise, nothing will come of your venture. Your task is to defeat them on the field where they have long felt like masters.

It's challenging but possible. Take advantage of the positive experience of successful competitors, and do not try to copy the failed ideas of those who have fallen out of the race. The past rarely returns on the Internet, and originality is not always rewarded.

The classic "survivor's mistake" is strengthening and improving the structural elements that survived and worked.

Its version on the Internet is different - when the creators of new projects do not take someone else's positive experience and, in pursuit of originality, repeat the decisions that have not survived and not worked, have led many projects to collapse.

Conformity is not always an elegant solution, though. But you have original content, right? It remains only to pack it in such a form that it will bring you success.

35.4. Practical advice for publishing content

Search engines don't like empty sites.

Here are some figures obtained at different times from different sources. These figures may not be entirely reliable or are already outdated, but they provide additional information for reflection.

Bing is starting to be nice to sites with more than 100 URLs.

The daily maximum of site URLs Bing accepts for indexing is 10000.

The daily maximum of site URLs accepted by Google for indexing is 200.

The minimum size of a site for approval in the Google AdSense system is 50 URLs of thematic content.

There is never too much content, you know?

So this is my practical advice.

Do not rush to open your site for indexing, and do not rush to promote it.

Create several dozens of posts, and don't leave empty categories on the site.

Write several dozens of posts that will be stored on your site as drafts.

After the site launch, you will have little time to work on new publications, and this reserve will be very useful to you. You will be able to publish (and promote!) pre-prepared posts regularly, which will positively affect site traffic.

Write and post content regularly; don't take long breaks.

Work according to the content plan, and do not stop adjusting and refining it. This is one of your main working papers!

Do you remember the chain? Plan - content - traffic - monetization.

We will talk a lot more about traffic, because this is inevitable, and I have something to tell you about.

As for monetization, this issue is entirely within your competence. We will also touch on this topic, but rather from the technical side. This project is not about business but about its technical support.

Nevertheless, we will have to touch on this topic soon to indicate the critical areas of technical work and to get an idea of the possible results.

36

Ways to monetize
your site

Website monetization is always a trendy and well-developed topic, but it is truly inexhaustible. It would seem, what could be new here?

It may be new to look at some aspects of this topic. To look directly, frankly, and pragmatically, without illusions.

36.1. What do we know about ways to monetize a site?

People who successfully monetize their sites know everything about monetization methods.

If you do not have such experience, then you do not know anything.

But you can always find information about it, right?

You just need to type a search query - and in the search feed, you will immediately see "a thousand ways to make money on the Internet," "69 most effective ways to monetize a site," and so on.

If you start studying all this information, you will only waste your time.

Get rid of illusions. No one will just share such super-valuable information as a description of how to become a millionaire without getting up from the couch.

The posts you find at the top of the search results are just text content made by someone to make money from contextual advertising. But that doesn't mean they aren't true.

The truth is that they are mostly useless for people who do not have experience in such work.

Instead of reading fascinating texts about how to make fabulous money without straining, just think. Think about what ways to make money on their own sites made people really rich.

You will quickly conclude that public recommendations and pep talks are useless. They are not specific and do not form the reader's real idea and vision of a process of generating income.

However, if you have never read such publications, read a few of them once to know what they are discussing.

Here, we will simply dot all the i's, and we will intentionally do this at the beginning of work on our future site, not at the end.

Of course, you can ask me why I'm going to show you ways to make money instead of making them myself.

This question is straightforward to answer. There are too many existing ways to make money on sites for it to be possible for one, even a very experienced and skilled person. I use only those that can be used based on creating your site. And this topic is so extensive that the issue of monetization takes up little space in it.

But you should give yourself the answer to this question even before you start working on your project, which will be based on a website.

36.2. Why the website is the backbone of many businesses today

To begin with, let's agree with the statement that people's lives have changed dramatically over the past decades.

Ways to Monetize Your Site

We stopped spending hours shopping and spending days in libraries, we only go to theaters for premiere screenings (less and less), and we stopped writing each other ordinary letters on paper and mailing Christmas cards.

Only that part of our life that cannot be transferred online has remained offline.

The same thing happened with business. It is not possible to move car production or pizza cooking online. But online (we mean, of course, websites) does a great job of displaying products, taking orders, receiving money from customers, and tracking the delivery of purchases.

Websites have converted to the front end of most businesses. The back end has been completely preserved in traditional industries in the form of plots of land built up with factories and warehouses.

It has also been partially preserved in its original form near the shopping centers.

The back end of all non-production, storage, and movement of physical goods businesses has shrunk to compact offices where most employees can successfully work remotely.

You may not know (and you do not know) where the server that broadcasts the series to your TV is physically located, what is the mailing address of the office where you took out an insurance policy for your dog through the website, and who is the writer whose digital book you are just downloaded to your reader.

Other users don't know this either, but they don't need to know.

It goes without saying, as well as the fact that any website that offers people something interesting, valuable, and affordable can collect as many visitors and customers as the most beautiful park and the best store on the Champs-Elysées never dreamed of.

Well, you get what I'm talking about, right?

If you have any product with a potential buyer, then your website is the perfect showroom, sales manager, and store for which there are no boundaries.

In short, all this is a compact solution that can be backed up at any moment on a regular flash drive or an SD card.

The website is a universal solution for organizing a business, available to anyone who wants to earn real money.

What is especially pleasant for business people is that creating a website requires a little investment of time and money. And what is the result?

Let's try to quickly understand the main thing based on the approximate average indicators obtained empirically.

36.3. Website monetization and its possible results

A great example is the well-known Amazon website. In 1994, Jeff Bezos decided to go into the business of selling books over the Internet, and the back end of his business was his garage.

The front end in the form of a website appeared already in 1995. The tireless work to improve service and expand the range of products led this business to an IPO in 1997. Well, you know the continuation.

What do you think Jeff Bezos could have achieved if, instead of building a perfectly functioning website and creating the most efficient global logistics system, he took out a loan to build a bookstore in Manhattan?

Would you like to continue with the example of Google? After all, initially, it was also just a website with a search spider.

Or maybe Facebook? YouTube? TikTok (yes, it's also a website; it's just that the client side was initially created as a mobile application, not a browser version)?

Perhaps the list of successfully monetized websites will be more compelling if you add to it agencies, travel companies, virtual offices of hotels and insurance companies, cryptocurrency exchanges, photo stocks, podcasting services, communities of language teachers, famous newspapers and magazines, supermarkets with common goods, or shops for animals?

The list can be continued indefinitely.

Each line of such a list, each separate item, will contain a website as the basis for working with a client, buyer, or customer, that is, with a person who pays money.

Connoisseurs count a dozen and a half ways to make money with Amazon alone, and most of them are simply impossible without the website.

"What do I have to do with this?" - You have the right to ask such a question, no doubt.

Yes. If you are not involved in it, you have nothing to do with making money with websites.

What does it take to monetize a website and make money with it?

As you already understand, you need three main components to monetize a website.

1. A product, service, digital asset, or valuable information, that is, something people need and for which they are willing to pay with their money or their time.
2. The site itself - which correctly offers one of the items listed in the previous paragraph.
3. Sufficient volume of targeted traffic so that potential customers, buyers, viewers, and readers visit your site in an amount that will be enough to generate the required income level.

If you have already decided on the first point and are ready to monetize your knowledge, experience, products, or works, consider the issue resolved.

If you haven't decided on the first point yet and continue to be attracted to publications with headlines like "33 win-win post ideas for your blog" or "99 types of posts that will grab the attention of readers", then you need to hurry.

The world is full of people who can choose their direction ahead of you and become competitors that you will need to catch up with.

The first point is inextricably linked to the third.

The actual usefulness and appeal of your products, services, recipes, and personal finance publications largely determine the minimum and maximum traffic you can get.

Everything is fair here: interesting content attracts visitors, profitable offers attract customers, and high-quality and affordable goods attract buyers.

The first and third points will receive their solutions because there is no business without supply and demand. Your offer can be poor or brilliant, and demand can be low, average, or hype.

As a result, you will earn little, or a lot, or make a great fortune.

But in any case, without a decision on the second point, that is, without your website, you will not earn anything at all. I mean - absolutely nothing!

36.4. Is a website required to make money?

The answer to this question is related to what you are going to make money on.

If you publish culinary recipes (or expert advice or entertaining anime of your production) and place advertisements and affiliate links on the pages of your site, then you cannot do without your site. Your site must be suitable for advertising and affiliate links.

If you write novels and sell them electronically and in print on Amazon (and elsewhere), then you need the site for representation purposes, to organize your fan club, and to link to the sale pages of your immortal masterpieces.

If you specialize in search engine optimization or SMM, then you need a site to accept applications from potential customers and accept payments from those who have already become actual customers.

If you sell digital resources (brochures, manuals, software, photo filters, or patterns for tiny dog vests), then you need a site to organize your online store.

When we discuss the practicalities of creating your site, we will look at themes and plugins that will allow you to create websites of these and other types. We will also take a closer look at the various ways to monetize.

Now, it is essential for us to clearly understand what is at stake.

You can say that you don't need a site because you have already started earning and making do with social media accounts (or other suitable platforms). That's where customers come to you, that's where they find you and your products, that's where they buy them, and you don't have to worry about anything.

Of course, you have the right to your unique point of view and your own approach to solving earnings issues. There are cases when people have been quite successfully earning in this way for several years.

Or they earned but then stopped (there are many such examples too).

Here's the difference (let's call social networks, trading systems, and mobile social messengers for short - platforms, and you - publisher).

1. Social platforms are not generally interested in users paying attention to your products and services and you personally. They need to keep users in their feeds and broadcast ads for which they get paid, not you. To retain users, they use various tricks and are very reluctant to share traffic, especially if your publications contain external links that can lead the visitor away.

2. Trading platforms are interested in the maximum number of sales, so they will show your competitors' products next to your product. The buyer will buy what he likes best, and if a competitor's offer seems more attractive to him, he can decide in favor of the competitor while on the page of your product. Trading systems are based on the competition of sellers, and you do not have any priority there.

3. Social messengers divide the whole world into advertisers and users. Users produce a tremendous amount of content, including some of the lowest quality, but this is more than enough to create an attractive info background for other users and for advertisers' ads. They are indifferent to all the rest - sellers, experts, publishers, writers, and others. They just need to keep these "others" in the number of users so as not to lose any of their audience because this is important for their relations with the advertiser. Therefore, social messengers provide minimal opportunities for monetization and sales.

4. Platforms consider anyone who tries to sell his products and services on their pages as a potential advertiser. Therefore, the publisher will inevitably expect an increase in the number of offers to take advantage of the advertising opportunities of the platform and, at best, the absence of an increase in free access to the audience. This must be understood: as soon as the publisher of a humble blog shows his intention to earn something, he immediately gets on the list of those from whom you can demand money.

5. Platforms do not encourage cross-linking. If you place your assets on the pages of one platform, this does not mean that you can freely place a link to it on other platforms. There are, of course, exceptions (for example, YouTube, which provides many options for sharing links to videos and within them).

6. Any platform may, at any time, for any reason, restrict the publisher's access to the audience, block publications, or even delete the account. Sometimes, publishers manage to defend their rights, but more often, the platform emerges victorious from any disputes. You must have heard horror stories about people losing accounts with hundreds of thousands and millions of subscribers. There can be many reasons for such events, and not all of them are on the platforms' conscience, but this does not make it easier for anyone.

If desired, this sad list can be lengthened and more detailed, but we have already said enough.

Your own site does not have these shortcomings and vulnerabilities. It may not be very, or, conversely, very well done, but it always:

- allows the publisher to fully retain visitors and manage their attention and behavior on the pages,
- demonstrates services and goods without restrictions and competition,

- contains and maintains all the tools and ways of earning that its owner provides,
- requires mandatory costs only to maintain the operation,
- can receive traffic from any sources that its owner deems fit to use,
- cannot be blocked by anyone and never if its owner did not violate any laws.

At present, your own website is the only reliable element in any earning system.

36.5. Actually, ways to monetize the site

We have already listed some of them above.

It remains to make only a few final remarks. Just to illustrate everything that was said above.

All estimates given are indicative. They allow only very rough estimates for comparing different possibilities.

36.5.1. How much can you earn on banner ads

The volume of the post or page - from 600 to 2000 words, 2-5 illustrations. The site has from 100 to 1000 posts. Google AdSense. Banner in the header, banner in the footer, and three banners in the body of the post. $5 to $10 per 1,000 on-page impressions.

A higher specific income is possible when working with other banner systems or in more expensive segments, up to $20 to $50 per 1,000 on-page impressions.

Let's assume reasonably achievable traffic when using free sources - up to 10 thousand page impressions daily. We get 50 - 100 dollars of income per day. If you can get more traffic, the income will naturally be higher.

Attempts to increase traffic by buying it, with that monetization way, are usually unprofitable.

36.5.2. How much can you earn on affiliate programs

The number and volume of publications are the same as in the previous paragraph. Traffic comes from free sources.

Sites that are affiliated with trading platforms or sites that sell goods and services should have a narrower thematic profile than sites that earn only from banner ads. This allows you to collect a more interested audience.

A typical response rate for posts with affiliate links and banners ranges from 1 to 5 percent.

If less than 1 percent of visitors make purchases through affiliate programs, then the site is gathering an insufficiently targeted audience.

If purchases are made by more than 5 percent, then this means that the published offer is very successful and perfectly matches the audience's interests.

There are times when the response reaches 10-20 percent, but this is rare.

Let's make an approximate calculation using the example of a product from the Amazon assortment (I wonder how much this assortment now exceeds 500 million items?).

So, a product with an average cost of $ 50, with a commission of 5% (depending on the category of the product and the number of sales), brings $ 2.5 from one purchase.

Out of a thousand visitors, with a response of 1 percent, we get 10 purchases. In total, every thousand visitors bring in $25, slightly higher than the income from banner advertising.

Publications on such sites should have a narrower thematic focus than in the case of earnings on banners. This complicates the work, but the possible effect, as we see, is higher.

Narrow topics associated with the need to write texts on specific products and services mean decreased traffic.

Therefore, bloggers and publishers often adhere to the following strategy: they add pages to their site dedicated to affiliate products and services and place both banners and affiliate links on these pages.

As a result, affiliate links bring additional income in relation to banners, which is only a few percent of the income received from placing banners.

Simply because there are much fewer pages with "affiliate" texts than other pages, and the percentage of the total site traffic is also small because of this.

Projects initially designed only to work with affiliate programs can count on a good income, but only in niches where successful competition is possible.

36.5.3. How much can you earn selling digital goods, books, consultations, and courses

The principles for calculating unit income are exactly the same as in the examples just considered. The main difference is that you do not receive a commission, but the whole declared price of your digital assets.

From this, we can conclude that such earnings are the most attractive. Many bloggers and authors earn tens and hundreds of thousands (and even millions) of dollars a year.

In fact, if one sale brings you $100, then with traffic of 1,000 visitors (10 sales is 1 percent of 1,000) per day, you can make up to $30,000 per month. Quite good, right?

Of course, you will have to share the income with the plugin authors or digital goods resellers, but in this case, it is they who receive their modest share, and the main income goes to you. Maybe you'll even be able to pay to advertise your products, and your business will be incredibly successful.

Everything depends on you. It remains only to finish work on your course, book, or collection of digital filters, build your own website, and start earning.

36.6. Conclusion

In this chapter, we approached the issues of website monetization from a somewhat unexpected angle. I guess now you have more clarity in understanding the very problem of monetization.

At this stage of work, we go from general to specific because each future site owner must know clearly what he intends to do and what result he should expect.

We'll look at the details later. Now, you need to understand that you can start this work, even alone and at a minimal cost.

Since your goal is to create a stable and fully controlled source of income for years to come, all your time, labor, and money are your investments in yourself, not someone else.

This is the most profitable type of investment invented by humanity.

37

What are cookies, why are they needed, and how to work with them

Everyone knows that cookies are some special data that either remain on the computer's hard drive after visiting a website or, on the contrary, are transferred somewhere. Most users know very little or no idea about this.

In this chapter, we'll quickly examine the most important things you should know without getting into unnecessary technical details.

37.1. Cookies are the standard technology

Cookies are not a malicious invention of hackers who pretend to be webmasters. This is a standard technology used in interacting with the web server (on which the site is located) with the browser (with which the visitor views the site pages).

The essence of what is happening is the following actions.

When a user opens a website page in his browser for the first time, along with the page itself displayed in the browser window, the server sends small files to the browser called "cookies."

These files are placed in a dedicated area of the browser's memory on the hard drive.

On subsequent visits to the same site, these cookies are transmitted to the web server along with the page's address the user wants to open.

As a result, the server always knows that this user has already been on this site, made some settings there, or logged in.

This is very convenient since none of us likes to enter a username and password or add the same item to the cart just because the server "forgot" this information during our coffee break.

By the way, cookies have different lifetimes, so a safe coffee break can vary from a few minutes to infinity.

37.2. Cookies are something without which the site may lose its functionality (and vice versa)

Some sites have work logic related to the sequence and composition of user actions.

If the site "forgets" the user's previous actions, it will not be able to determine his next actions.

If you block such a site from using cookies, you may not be able to use that site.

Therefore, it is not recommended to disable all cookies, and the possibility of their complete or selective prohibition or use is available and not always needed.

Essentials About Cookies

First Visit to the Website

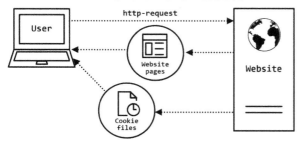

Next Visits to the Website

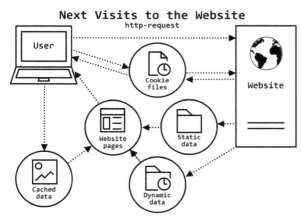

Sometimes, there are entirely different problems. For example, if a user enters some of their data into an order form and then finds an error that cannot be corrected, they will have to delete the cookies related to this site and fill out the form again. This usually indicates that the page with the data entry form is not made well enough.

37.3. Cookies are sometimes insecure

Cookies are the very first, oldest, and most imperfect technology for exchanging data about the interaction between the browser and the server. It appeared back in 1994.

It is quite natural to assume that over the long years of the existence of this technology, its capabilities have been studied and used not only by conscientious and law-abiding people. Fraudsters were also interested in this technology from the very beginning of its existence and continue to be interested now.

The main thing you should know is that if the site uses the secure SSL data transfer protocol, that is, the addresses of its pages do not start with HTTP, but with HTTPS, then there is no danger.

Hackers can steal cookies if the site runs on the HTTP protocol, mainly if you work in a public free WiFi zone. If you are just looking at the news or exciting recipes and have not entered any logins and passwords anywhere, nothing threatens you, even when using HTTP. But it is better to know that in public places, you should not use public networks if you decide to go to your bank page and make some payment.

37.4. Cookies are something that the site owner cannot directly influence

If you create a WordPress site and install a plugin for authorization through social networks, or your users will log in the standard way to comment on posts, your site will undoubtedly use cookies.

If you are administering a WordPress site from your computer, cookies on your hard drive will allow you not to enter an administrator login and password for two weeks.

If you connect the Google Analytics system to the site, it will use its cookies.

If you connect the Google Adsense system to the site, it will use its cookies.

I think you already understood everything.

When you create a website, you cannot prevent Google Analytics or the forum administration plugin from setting cookies on users' hard drives.

You can only make decisions about using specific components on your site. It is only necessary to comply with simple requirements.

37.5. The site must comply with the requirements for the use of cookies

Most importantly, it is impossible to install cookies on their computers without the consent of users and, moreover, transfer their data to third parties.

By the way, the latter is the main requirement of the California Consumer Privacy Act (CCPA) and other regional laws and regulations.

The European GDPR is global, and over 100 countries have issued their formal requirements. This may seem like unnecessary bureaucracy for some and a legally significant circumstance for others.

What should a simple owner of an ordinary information site or a thematic blog do? How do we meet the requirements of all these acts, laws, and regulations, the number of which will only increase with time?

Please don't be scared - it's not too difficult. You only need to follow three rules.

1. Do not use components that may allow the illegal use of cookies. Only install plugins and extensions from official sources on your site. Services from Google, themes, and plugins from the official WordPress site are fairly reliable sources where you will find absolutely everything you need for your site.
2. Provide website visitors with information about the use of cookies. It would be appropriate to set aside a section for this information on the mandatory page of your site's "Privacy Policy." To do this, you will have to look into your browser settings and make a list of cookies (don't forget to exclude cookies related to administrator access to the WordPress system).
3. The first time you visit your site (and subsequent visits, usually after the cookie expires in 1 year), you must warn the visitor that your site uses cookies. Any specialized plugin for WordPress can handle this task. Of course, if your site is very interactive and uses authorization, stores user accounts, sells goods, and accepts payments, then you must use a more professional plugin. Still, you will know what to do when you require such a need.

Detailed first-hand information about cookies can be found here. *https://www.aboutcookies.org/* .

You can find out exactly which cookies a particular site stores on your hard drive and, if you wish, delete them using a special extension for the Google Chrome browser or directly in the browser itself - Menu/ Settings/ Privacy and Security/ Cookies and other site data/ See all cookies and site data/ (*chrome://settings/siteData*, start typing the domain name in the search bar at the top right of the window). If you are not afraid of technical information, this source from Google may be useful. *https://developer.chrome.com/docs/devtools/storage/cookies/* .

38

How to work
with cPanel

The cPanel console is explicitly designed for casual users, not advanced techies. Therefore, cPanel is the main tool of every website owner.

This is a straightforward, clear, and convenient Linux hosting control panel. The first version of cPanel was released back in 1996 and has been continuously improved ever since.

This console has been so successful that in all these years, no other hosting management product has been able to compete sufficiently (although, of course, there are excellent hosting management consoles for different operating systems and special applications).

The possibilities of cPanel are extensive, and you will thoroughly familiarize yourself with them in due time. Now, we must make a small overview and list the most commonly used features.

Login to cPanel is organized differently for different hosting companies. Usually, a separate login and password are provided for logging into cPanel (not those used to register and enter the primary hosting site, but additional ones), as well as entry by clicking on the panel logo in the hosting account interface. Just keep that in mind.

38.1. The appearance of the cPanel interface

The cPanel interface has built-in visual presentation controls. Simply put, your host can pre-configure the appearance of the cPanel interface following their ideas of beauty.

Here, we provide screenshots that show the classic appearance of the cPanel interface. This type of design is traditionally called "Basic."

If you want to use this particular type of design, you can activate it through the menu item marked in the screenshot.

38.2. Function blocks - sections of the cPanel menu system

After logging into the cPanel interface, you will see an extensive menu organized by sections on the left side of the screen and an information sidebar on the right.

All elements have simple and understandable names, and all that is required of you is to know the basics of hosting management specifics and understand that all your actions immediately impact your site.

To learn and understand all this is quite simple. We will proceed from the fact that you have a website, and it is connected and accessible by a domain name.

All features available in cPanel are grouped by topic.

Remember that many of the features available to you in cPanel you will never need. The fact is that this system is redundant simply because, in the process of development, it received all the possibilities that could be implemented.

Many tasks are solved in other ways; many functions are unnecessary when working with WordPress: many features are simply obsolete and traditionally preserved, and many tools are rarely required.

38.3. What features of cPanel should be used

Here's what you'll need first:
- FILES/ File manager - to work with the files of your site, it goes without saying,
- DATABASES/ MySQL Databases - to create a database and its user,
- SECURITY/ SSL/TLS - to connect access via the HTTPS (SSL) protocol,
- SOFTWARE/ Select PHP Version - to connect the required PHP version (rarely required),
- SOFTWARE/ Cloudflare - for connecting CDN (if you have access and your need),
- DOMAINS/ Zone Editor - for editing DNS records (may not be required),
- EMAIL/ Email Accounts - to create mailboxes and access mail (if necessary).

Once your site is up and running, you will use these components:
- METRICS/ Errors - to check for server errors (rare),
- METRICS/ Resource Usage - to control compliance with hosting restrictions,
- METRICS/ Visitors - to search for intruders and check the correct operation of the site,
- FILES/ File manager - for current work with files and backups,
- DATABASES/ phpMyAdmin - for working with backups.

If everything works correctly and you make no mistakes while creating and setting up the site, you will likely never need the rest of the features. Or they will be required in some critical situations, for the resolution of which it is better to use the services of technical support specialists.

In any case, your curiosity is not a strong enough argument for experimenting with the cPanel interface to see "what happens when you click here."

In addition, you, like any site owner, will have many other equally exciting things to do and very little time for such research.

Please note that I am not mentioning the features related to installing and configuring WordPress, creating backups, and restoring sites from backups.

These are critical reliability tasks, and I highly recommend doing them manually.

This is no more difficult than clicking on beautiful icons, but it guarantees complete control over the processes and results. I'll show you how it's done when we get to this topic.

Elements of the cPanel interface that correspond to the listed features are marked in the screenshot.

Your system may have function blocks in a different order, but you can swap them around if you want. Just drag and drop.

Also, function blocks can be collapsed to the header or expanded to the list of icons by clicking on the "-" and "+" signs (also noted in the screenshot).

Capabilities of the Hosting Console
(main features on the example of cPanel)

FILES/ File Manager

Create • Delete • Edit • View • Upload • Download • Compress • Extract

DATABASES

Create • Delete • Edit • phpMyAdmin • Users • Passwords • Permissions

METRICS

Visitors • Errors • Statistics • Resource Usage • Bandwidth

DOMAINS

Addon Domains • Subdomains • Redirects • Zone Editor • Site Publisher

SECURITY

SSL/ TLS • Leech Protection • Hotlink protection • IP Blocker

EMAIL

Accounts • Forwarders • Autoresponders • Mailing Lists • Spam Filters

SOFTWARE

PHP Version • Apps Installer • Apps Manager • WP Manager

As you can see, the interface is quite friendly. To finally believe this, look at the screenshot of File Manager. It is unlikely that you will find any completely incomprehensible words in it.

Remember that this interface works with both left-click and right-click context menus. Everything is simple.

In more detail, we will discuss performing specific tasks using File Manager and other cPanel components as needed, explaining all the steps.

It's much easier and more efficient than explicitly learning cPanel in great detail, most of which you're unlikely to ever need. And if you ever need them, you will already know you have become a real professional. Therefore, we continue with you on the path we began to move along.

Your goal of creating the website that works for you just got closer.

39

Website promotion and user data

Website promotion today is no less critical process than its creation.

The interest of the target audience and its loyalty depend on the site's quality, and the implementation of the project goals, including income, depends on the effectiveness of the promotion.

It is the goals of the project that determine the nature and methods of promoting the website. Let's start with their consideration. We will omit the details that are superfluous at the moment. In the future, they will be considered in detail and without omissions.

39.1. The purpose of the web project and ways to promote the website

Every website has potential and an actual audience.

The potential audience cannot be more than the total number of people worldwide who, in principle, can visit your site and understand what information is published on it. These are the people who understand the language of the site.

Further, the division of the potential audience into clusters begins - according to interests, gender and age, place of residence, and other characteristics.

Is it interesting for you? Hardly.

All this data has long been processed by specialists and can be obtained without difficulty, but not always for free.

The main thing is to understand that your site has a potential audience.

And one more thing you need to understand: the set of promotion methods available to you is limited, and your competitors have it, too.

Each promotion method includes attracting new visitors (advertising, publications, search, all possible ways of informing about the project) and fixing interested visitors (in the form of full-fledged leads, email lists, subscribers in a social network, etc.) to further work with them.

In the early years of the website era, the promotion cost was low, and visitors could only bookmark a site's address or subscribe to a mailing list.

Both methods were not very reliable, but there were no others.

Browser bookmarks for an ordinary user quickly turned into an impenetrable jungle, and mailing lists brought the site owner to the blacklist of mail spammers (system administrators had to do something!).

Today, the cost of promotion varies from zero to infinity, and there are many ways to remember the address of a site or become a regular reader, and they are also not all available for free.

Here are the main ways to attract new visitors:

- search traffic
- direct advertising,
- placement of announcements of publications with direct links (blog platforms, social networks),
- placement of special formats with direct links (hybrid platforms - Pinterest, Youtube, Instagram),
- placement of special formats with indirect links (podcasts, Q&A services, forums),
- placement of special formats with direct and indirect links in special services (link in bio, instant messengers, message publishing services, guest blog posts).

Each site owner can find the features that give it advantages.

If you are a master at video editing, you can start a YouTube channel and use it to solve the problem of getting traffic to the site and monetizing your video channel.

If you are a good writer, you will surely be able to find ways to use blogging platforms effectively. This is not the main problem.

The main problem is the relationship between the cost of getting one site visitor and the benefit their visit will bring you.

The solution to this problem is the answer to the advisability of promoting the site in one way or another.

Here's the epic formula: $P = S/N - V/M.$

If the value of P is greater than zero, then you make a profit.

If the value of P is less than zero, then you take a loss.

Guessed? If not, then here is the decoding of the designations (for some time, for example, for a month):

S - your total cost of attracting N visitors to the site (advertising costs, or the cost of your life support, including electricity bills, or the sum of payments to hired freelancers - choose what you need),

V - total income from the project,

M is the number of site visitors who paid you.

You can slightly transform and simplify this simple formula to the difference between income and expenses for the period, but this does not change the essence of the matter and distracts attention from the most important thing - working with visitors.

All other details of the process of attracting visitors, including various indicators like CTR, CPM, RPM, and the like, are good for detailed analysis of what is happening when your site is ready, working, and selling what it should sell. Then, the accounting of returned visitors, remarketing, and other helpful inventions of humanity will be applicable.

The goal pursued by your project should always be fulfilled: the real benefit from one average site visitor should exceed the actual cost of attracting this visitor.

It's banal and obvious, you say?

Nobody argues with this. But you will be surprised that most site owners rarely consider it. They just do not have time - the site requires constant care and attention, falling traffic needs to be raised, conversion must be high, and, in general, many various issues need attention and solutions.

While there is no site or it does not yet have traffic, there are simple truths. Here they are.

39.2. How to choose a website promotion method

39.2.1. Website promotion in search

If you manage to get to the first line of Google search results for any search query, you are guaranteed a response from 10 to 25 percent of the total number of visitors who enter this query. Top queries can be entered hundreds of thousands and millions of times a month. This means that for such a request, your site can receive hundreds and thousands of visits per day.

Website Promotion

Just keep in mind that your competitors have the same information. And many of them are already at the top of the search results. To stand next to them or to rise above them, you will have to put in a lot of effort to create high-quality content, pay for the services of an SEO specialist, and spend a lot of time waiting for the result.

This method is appropriate if you create a large amount of quality content and publish it often.

A similar approach works when you use hybrid platforms for promotion. For example, when publishing a video on YouTube, you can differentiate yourself from your competitors with the help of a video sequence, which is impossible in a regular text search.

By the way, video materials are independently involved in the search and can bring traffic to the site directly from the search

Collecting User Data

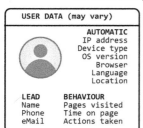
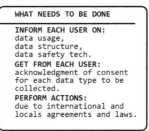

results. This way of promotion gives results that can last for months and years. That is why promoting a website in search is perhaps the most important way.

39.2.2. Website promotion on social networks and hybrid platforms

Efforts to promote the website on social networks and the pages of hybrid platforms (Pinterest and various social blogging platforms) give faster results.

However, the performance of free publications with links to pages of websites and blogs in such traffic sources has declined significantly in recent years.

Many of this promotion method's features are free. If your subject is of interest and the level of incoming traffic suits you, then this is a good working option.

With such a promotion, the results practically do not accumulate - placed posts with links can usually bring noticeable traffic for no more than a few days, after which it drops to almost zero. An essential advantage of this method of promotion is the ability to create a community of regular readers and subscribers.

39.2.3. Website promotion with paid advertising

This method does not only apply to buying advertising traffic on search engines and social networks. For the money, you can place guest posts and links with invitations to the sites of famous bloggers. It is advisable to use this method at the initial stage of the site's life, immediately after its launch, and when selling rather expensive goods and services is advisable.

As a rule, paid website advertising requires the participation of experienced consultants and is never bought at random. Therefore, if you decide to spend money promoting a website this way, you must also think carefully about all aspects of such work.

In any case, when choosing any way to promote websites, you must solve the problem of collecting and storing user information. You need to "preserve" the audience. This is the most critical result of website promotion!

39.3. How to collect, store and use audience information

1. If you are collecting information in the form of "leads," that is, names, phone numbers, and email addresses, using a landing page on your website, then you will need to comply with additional requirements for the confidentiality and security of the processing of personal data of your visitors.
2. If you use specialized services to store leads, which, for example, provide services for the sale of digital goods, then a significant part of the requirements for confidentiality and security of processing your visitors' data will not apply to you and your site, but to the services that you use. However, you are also responsible for complying with these requirements.
3. If you collect and store information in the form of a list of subscribers on a social network, then all requirements for the security and confidentiality of users' data apply to this social network. This, of course, does not entitle anyone to the unauthorized use of such information. We are talking only about technical measures to ensure privacy and security.

That is a very important point. Users understand that their data must be protected, and you should also be aware of this. This is especially important when using information already collected about your audience. You need:

• provide the possibility for the user to unsubscribe and receive your marketing information (letters, messages, offers, news),
• ensure that users are informed about the purposes of collecting information and obtaining consent from each of them,
• organize the storage of information about users, excluding access to it by third parties,
• comply with international and local requirements for working with personal information.

Important advice: When promoting a site, do not forget to provide users with the ability to save information about it in instant messengers, bookmarkers, and browser bookmarks. Be sure to provide widgets, links, and buttons intended for this on the pages of the site.

40

Website
Life Cycle Stages

The life cycle of a website is most often viewed from the point of view of its developer. You can find many publications where the last stage of the site's life cycle is referred to as its launch, and much less often, the operation stage is mentioned.

Everything that happens after the website's launch is usually not discussed in any way. We think this is wrong. Any owner of a "real" offline business will say that with the launch of an office or a store, everything is just beginning, and they will be absolutely right.

The same goes for websites. In general, we will try to give a complete picture of the site's life cycle.

40.1. Competitor website analysis and idea generation

Behind every website are real people who have specific goals and interests. They have already done a lot of work, created their websites, operated them, and received income.

There is nothing wrong with learning from the experiences of others.

You can not copy the elements of the business that are protected by law, and everything else is a great source of inspiration for the creator and future owner of his website.

The easiest way to form an idea is to "do it the same way" as one of the competitors. But this is not a very reasonable way in all respects. If you just copy and imitate, you will forever remain in the role of catching up.

The most reasonable option for generating ideas is to "do the same but with one difference." Marketers like to call this difference "lateral shift" and have built a huge number of theories and methods around this term.

The essence of this has not changed, and you need to understand why.

One difference from the competitor is that it is a very convenient tuning tool that is easy to advertise and easy to explain to a potential buyer. If this difference gives a clear advantage to the buyer, then he will choose you without hesitation.

This is very important - decision-making and purchases on the Internet are made very quickly.

If your idea differs from that of a successful competitor in several ways, then it will be more difficult for you to convey its benefits to consumers.

If your idea is so original that it has no analogs in the market, then you are waiting for either a huge success or a complete failure.

Website Life Cycle

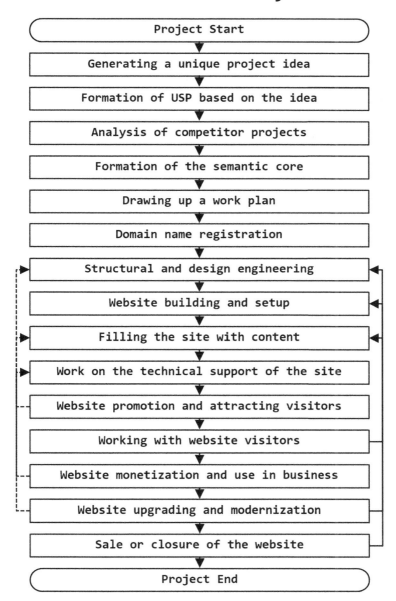

In general, the technology of creating an idea for a website is essentially no different from the technology of creating an idea for any business.

Look at the marketing material. It may help you clarify the situation.

40.2. Forming a proposal based on an idea

Forming a proposal based on an idea.

Simple sentences like "buy my product because it costs the same, but it's better" or "buy my product because it's the same, but cheaper" no one can be convinced of anything these days.

Your task is to form a technically feasible proposal based on the idea you created in a form that is attractive to visitors and suitable for use in creating a project.

In the form of a proposal, your idea should take on a practical form and become suitable for discussion with the people to whom you intend to entrust it.

For example, if your idea is "trading books," the offer is "buying and selling antiquarian books online to Latin language lovers."

Just refine the idea and add technical information to it.

40.3. The general plan of work related to the website

Further actions will be connected not only with your observations of the world around you but also with the thoughts that arise in your head.

You will need to bring each subsequent step to implementation - in the form of documents, a domain name, a working site, a list of customers, or a profit.

If you decide to create a website and launch your own business, then you should not neglect this stage.

Take any guide on writing business plans, find documents that govern online business in your country, and write your plan. In the future, this will be your main working document, which you will supplement and correct.

Write down all subsequent stages in it and record the time and money spent on each of them. If you do not do this, then in the future, it will be extremely difficult for you to analyze the actions performed and find your own mistakes.

Do not rely on your memory and your intuition. Record what is happening and plan for the future.

40.4. Website design

This is the most creative stage, and it can take an incredibly long time and lead to the formation of unrealistic requirements and unrealizable technical ideas.

To prevent this from happening, just look at competitors' sites, find out what components they use, explore the interfaces, and find a place in this whole picture for the features and differences of your project.

Fix the results in the form of thumbnails of typical pages of the future site. Pencil drawings or sketches made in any program of your choice are suitable. Already at this stage, unnecessary or questionable components or blocks will either disappear by themselves or take on a completely realizable appearance.

Separately record the description of the data that will be used on your site. If you will publish only standard information materials (illustrations and articles), then this is not necessary. If you intend to create and use any non-standard formats, be sure to record information about the purpose, composition, and length of information fields.

When choosing a theme and plugins for your site, this information will be very useful to you, as themes and plugins often apply length restrictions, for example, to titles, subtitles, descriptions, abbreviations, and other elements.

Try also to capture information about the intended actions of the user and the corresponding changes in the browser window. So you get the first idea about the functioning of your future site, discard the unnecessary, and save the necessary.

40.5. Website creation

Actually, it is the embodiment of all ideas and plans.

Buying a domain name, buying and setting up hosting, installing WordPress, installing a theme and plugins, setting up, creating drafts of publications, a menu system, templates and blanks for pages and posts, test illustrations, feedback forms, and all the rest.

As a result, you will get a completely ready-to-work website with no content.

This is a rather ambiguous moment in terms of psychological perception: you have already implemented all your ideas, you can see the site, it almost works, and you even applied all your design decisions to it and placed a beautiful logo on it, which took so much creative effort, but the site is closed to visitors because there is no content on it.

But you imagine the content as something already ready, and some of the texts have already been written.

But!

You don't have all the texts ready; rather, almost all the texts are not ready, there are no illustrations, not all external links have been collected, the posts to which internal links should lead are not ready, and there are not enough social media profiles (and the existing ones are still empty).

So, it's time for you to move on to the next step.

40.6. Filling the website with content

You already have a plan, right? And you know exactly how much and what kind of content you need to create by the time the site is launched.

It is very good. Because time is running out, calendar cells change each other, and you need to be in time for the start of the business (tourist, Christmas) season with a large enough margin for your site to make its first steps on time.

Maybe you even planned the start of an advertising campaign?

Then you have no time to waste (just like me when I wrote this text).

Filling a website with content is one of the stages in the life cycle of a website that does not end when it is launched. Adding new and editing already published content is necessary constantly and regularly until the end of the life of the website.

40.7. Maintenance and technical support of the website

Once you've installed WordPress and your site has displayed its home page for the first time in your browser window, you're probably going to have a strong urge to back it up immediately.

It's a good idea.

You should always have a backup.

In 2 copies, no less.

Backing up and restoring a site after faults and crashes, transferring a site to other hosts, updating WordPress, themes, and plugins, editing styles, adding widgets, optimizing speed, and much more - this is normal.

This is work that begins at the moment the site is launched and ends only at the moment the project is closed. This is a job that guarantees the existence of your business.

40.8. Website promotion

Of course, the promotion work will end only when you decide to close the project (and start the next one).

You can start this work even before the launch of the site, creating and developing, for example, thematic pages and communities of interest in social networks.

If you intend to close one project and start the next, then using the audience you already have may not be a bad idea.

In general, after you have started to promote your own projects and have gathered a loyal audience, you certainly do not want to lose it completely when launching new projects. Sometimes, it turns out that conducting several projects at once is very useful for each of them.

The main thing is not to stop this work.

40.9. Working with website visitors

Even if your site does not sell anything but simply displays ads in the texts of posts, you will work with its audience.

You'll have to control session parameters and figure out how user behavior changes, how much time they spend on your site, where they go to your pages from, what countries they live in, and what search queries they are most interested in.

If your site sells goods or services, then you will have to deal with individual work with your buyers and customers.

It is very good. If you need to communicate with visitors, then your project is alive.

Of course, you will have to do this work during the entire life of the project.

40.10. Closing or selling the project

Of course, each of us wishes success and long life for our projects.

But life develops and flows according to its own laws, and sooner or later, you may have to part with the project and close or sell your site.

This is fine. And we, of course, wish your project a successful fate at all stages of the life cycle, including this last stage.

We mention this stage now just for the sake of completeness.

Just in case, remember the wording "exit strategy."

Afterword

So, you have taken the first steps toward your website. Self-hosted, with your own domain name, on a real host.

Let's summarize.

To begin with, we will simply list very briefly what you have learned from this book.

Imagine listing your new knowledge as a cloud of tags, each corresponding to a specific topic.

Site name, domain, domain name, TLD, SLD, domain name registration, domain name protection, hosting, hosting options, hosting selection, domain name delegation, delegation verification, hosting resources, cPanel, server access, site types, site builders, CMS, WordPress, site design, site content, content types, content placement, site reputation, traffic, visitors, speed, SEO, technical SEO, onsite SEO, offsite SEO, semantic core, frontend, backend, WordPress installation, site management, WordPress theme, WordPress plugin, WordPress pattern, classic editor, block editor, content plan, content publishing, monetization, monetization methods, cookies, website promotion, promotion methods, life cycle.

This is just a simple listing.

All the words that we have just listed are no longer just words for you.

Now you know their meaning. You know the relationship between words and meanings.

This subject has ceased to be a stranger to you.

Now you know what practical steps you need to take to create your own website. You know how they are interconnected and in what sequence you need to act.

It became clear to you what the site consists of, how it works, and what it can be. You are able to analyze your needs and make a choice of the type of site you need consciously, based on your own understanding of the tasks that the site should solve.

You understand the key concepts that affect the fate of the site and can determine the measure of its future success. For you, there are no more mysteries in the special terms that the participants in the market for website creation services operate with.

You know in what sequence you need to create and how to promote the site. You know the technologies and tools to solve all the problems that you may need.

You have a general vision of the picture of all stages of the site life cycle, and you know about the existence of formal and official requirements for it.

You know a lot about ways to monetize websites.

Now you are able to formulate the business goal of your project, you know where to start, and you know what needs to be done next.

It's like getting behind the wheel of a car for the first time in your life. You already know how it works and what it is for; you have been told how to use it, and you have read the rules of the road traffic and studied road signs.

Now, you have to drive a real car for the first time on your own. You have to practice. Your project should be born and start to live.

We will do it together in the second book of the series.

About the author

André Zon is a professional programmer and a specialist in the development and quality assurance of software and information products.

In the early 1990s, he was among the first developers of educational and entertainment multimedia applications released on CD-ROM. In 1997, he began developing websites for significant periodicals. He took and continues to take part in many projects in different countries of the world.

Participation in developing dozens of systems, including websites and mobile applications, allowed André to accumulate tremendous practical experience and a large amount of knowledge at a high expert level. He considers his primary competence to be the ability to see projects as a whole and to organize work so that each project is completed on time and with high quality.

Own developments in content management systems (CMS) and extensive practical experience allowed the author to understand and learn much about creating websites. André perfectly knows what must be done step-by-step to create a successful website.

Many years of interaction with customers, website owners, and specialists in various business areas has allowed him to deeply understand the needs and problems of people and companies that need to create their own websites and organize their successful work in the future.

The accumulated practical experience and multilateral knowledge of the author became the basis of a detailed guide to the creation and subsequent use of websites, which is intended for people without special training.

More information, links to social profiles, and a contact form can be found on the author's homepage at https://andrezon.com. Please scan this QR code to open it.

www.ingramcontent.com/pod-product-compliance
Lightning Source LLC
LaVergne TN
LVHW051241050326
832903LV00028B/2517